# WORKING WITH PEOPLE I WANT TO PUNCH IN THE THROAT

## CANTANKEROUS CLIENTS, MICROMANAGING MINIONS, AND OTHER SUPERCILIOUS SCOURGES

### JEN MANN

THROAT PUNCH MEDIA, LLC

*This book is dedicated to everyone
toiling in cubicle farms everywhere.
This book is also dedicated to Randall.
I might not agree with how you motivated me,
but you sure motivated me.*

# CONTENTS

Also by Jen Mann                                              vii

Author's Note                                                  ix

PEOPLE I WANT TO PUNCH IN THE                                  xi
THROAT: THE INTEROFFICE MEMO
EDITION

Cast of Characters                                             xv

Introduction                                                  xix

THE EARLY YEARS                                                 1

1. HOW I BECAME THE RICHEST LOSER                               2
IN JUNIOR HIGH AND THE ENVY OF
ALL THE NEIGHBORHOOD SOCCER
MOMS

2. THAT AWKWARD MOMENT WHEN                                    12
YOUR COLLEGE ADVISOR TELLS YOU
TO LOSE YOUR DREAMS AND MAJOR
IN YOUR MRS.

3. NEPOTISM AND POCKET                                         25
PROTECTORS: MY FIRST REAL JOB

THE NEW YORK YEARS                                             39

4. THANKS FOR INTERVIEWING ME                                  41
AND MY HIDEOUS NOSE

5. IF YOU WORK IN THE DUNGEON, CAN                             54
YOU STILL CALL IT A DREAM JOB?

6. AND THEN DOROTHY WENT TO                                    75
WORK FOR MARY POPPINS

7. I DO NOT GET PAID ENOUGH FOR                                85
THIS SHIT

8. YOU CAN'T FIRE ME—I QUIT!                                   95

9. WATCH OUT, I'M A VERY DANGEROUS                            106
KOALA BEAR

10. I WAS WRONG BEFORE—I DON'T GET          116
PAID ENOUGH FOR THIS SHIT

THE REAL ESTATE YEARS                        129
11. TOWELS ARE FOR CLOSERS                   131
12. THE TOUGHEST JOB I'LL EVER LOVE          140
13. "HEY MAN, DO YOU THINK I'M DOING         156
THIS FOR MY HEALTH?" AND OTHER
THINGS I'D LIKE TO YELL AT PEOPLE
14. THIS IS GOING TO BE GREAT OR             165
WE'RE GOING TO GET DIVORCED
15. HEY LADY, YOU WISH YOU HAD               176
ANYTHING NICE ENOUGH TO STEAL

THE WRITING YEARS                            193
16. THANK YOU, ELF ON THE SHELF, YOU         195
LITTLE BASTARD

Acknowledgments                             213
About the Author                            215
Also by Jen Mann                            217

ALSO BY JEN MANN

My Lame Life: Queen of the Misfits

People I Want to Punch in the Throat: Competitive
Crafters, Drop-Off Despots, and Other Suburban Scourges

Spending the Holidays with People I Want to Punch in the
Throat: Yuletide Yahoos, Ho-Ho-Humblebraggers, and
Other Seasonal Scourges

But Did You Die?

I Just Want to Be Perfect

I STILL Just Want to Pee Alone

I Just Want to Be Alone

I Just Want to Pee Alone

Just a Few People I Want to Punch in the Throat (Vols. 1-6)

## AUTHOR'S NOTE

All of the names and identifying characteristics of the people who appear in this book have been changed to protect the good, the bad, and the ugly. So if you think you can see yourself in these pages, please be assured that you are most certainly wrong. These are my stories and this is how I remember them.

# PEOPLE I WANT TO PUNCH IN THE THROAT: THE INTEROFFICE MEMO EDITION

**McJob: (noun) A low-paying job that requires little skill and provides little opportunity for advancement.**
*Merriam-Webster Dictionary*

**The micromanagers who aren't even my managers.** Stop it. You're not the boss of me. Literally.

**The know-it-alls.** I get it. You're very smart. You have all the answers. Do you have the answer to this question: Why are you so annoying?

**Mandatory lunch meetings.** The only thing worse is a five a.m. conference call. Whoever schedules these are dicks. We took a vote. We all hate you.

**The person who brings tuna to the mandatory lunch meeting.** Thanks for making the conference room smell like dirty vagina.

**Meetings to plan a meeting to plan a meeting.** Also known as the circle jerk of the business world.

**The buzzwords.** "Deep dive," "circle up," "corporate synergy," "disrupt," "pivot," "thought leadership." It's all meaningless word salad. Put a pin in these words already.

**The busiest people ever.** I'm sorry, did I ask what you were working on? Oh, that's right, I DON'T CARE!

**That one guy who asks a question when the meeting is wrapping up.** WTF, guy?! We were almost done and you ruined it with your dumb fucking question that you probably already knew the answer to, but you just like to hear the sound of your own voice.

**The yukkers.** I see you following the boss around, yukking it up over every single one of his jokes. He's not even funny. Also, there's some shit on your nose.

**The reply-all people.** Go kill yourself.

**That guy who trashes the break room.** Your mom doesn't work here. Clean up after yourself, you pig.

**Whoever jammed the printer and didn't fix it.** I have a quarterly update I'd like to jam up your ass.

**The coasters.** How do you do it? You do *nothing* but the boss loves you. I hate you, but I also kind of bow down, because that's impressive.

**The mansplainers.** Here's what you fellas need to understand: thanks for taking what I said and regurgitating it back to me like I'm a small, dimwitted child. Your help was incalculable.

**Company-wide happy hours.** I barely want to work with you. I definitely don't want to have a beer with you.

**The Ivy Leaguers.** You do know every sentence doesn't have to start with, "When I was at Princeton..."?

**The martyrs.** You get sick days—use one. Stop dragging your sniffling, snorting, coughing, sneezing ass to work and infecting the rest of us. You're not that important.

**The commute.** I'm exhausted and stressed out before I even get to the cubicle farm.

**Loud talkers.** Oh my God, shut up! No one wants to hear your conversation with your doctor about the weird thing on your foot.

**People who sit on my desk.** Ew. Don't put your pooper on my planner.

**My paycheck.** Are you fucking kidding me?

**Clients.** They won't take your advice, but blame you for their shitty results.

**Wearing pants.** I do my best work in pajamas.

# CAST OF CHARACTERS

**Jen: Me.** Unless you know me from pre-1990, in which case I'm Jenni. Notice, it's not "Jennifer." My parents didn't name me Jennifer. That would have been too trendy. They wanted to be original when naming me the most popular name of the decade. So they went wild and put their own flavor on a classic by putting an "i" on the end, thereby killing all possibility of me becoming a heart surgeon. Think about it, who would you trust more to do your bypass: Dr. Mandi or Dr. Amanda? When you have a name that ends in an adorable "i" that can only be written with a heart for a dot, it guarantees you'll end up on either the pole or the keyboard. Luckily, I chose the keyboard. I'm sarcastic, grumpy, and sweary. You've been warned.

**The Hubs:** I'm married to Ebeneezer, but I usually call him the Hubs. You can call him the Hubs too. Everyone does. He's used to it. He's Chinese and I'm Caucasian, sometimes that's helpful to know. He's a cheap bastard who can be a tad antisocial and a bit of a know-it-all, but he treats me like gold, so he's my lobster. The foundation of our marriage is built on relentless teasing of one another, constant griping, and the knowledge that no one else could stand us, so we'd better make this work. Oh yeah, I forgot about love. I meant to say love is the foundation of our marriage—the love of bickering.

**Gomer and Adolpha (aged twelve and ten at the writing of this book):** Before you have a hissy fit and sit down to write me a nasty letter about my children's horrible names, just stop. *Of course* those aren't their real names. Come on. Do you think I'm an idiot? Their real names are actually worse, but I can't take the ridicule so I just made up what I consider to be horrific names for them. I get the most hate mail about their names. Why? Because people can't read.

**My Mom:** For most of my childhood my mom was a stay-at-home mom. She is a classic overachiever who treats shopping, decorating, and housekeeping like full-time high-paying jobs. She once worked in a clothing store but had to quit because she convinced herself that with her discount it was almost like the store was paying her to shop. I'm not sure if it's related or not, but the month after my mother was forced to quit, the retailer reported record losses in earnings.

**My Dad:** AKA "Sugar Daddy." My dad has held countless job titles throughout the years. He's that faithful employee who moves every eighteen months for a promotion until he finally lands at the mother ship. I don't think he has a clue how much money he's made. He's that guy who just hands over his paycheck to his wife and hopes there's something left for him at the end of the month. What little he's able to squirrel away, he gives to his grandchildren. Whenever my kids get home from spending time with him, I turn them upside down and shake them so I can add to their college funds.

**C.B.:** My younger, smarter brother. Also a fake name. In fact, you can just assume that every name you read in this book besides Jen or Jenni is not real. C.B. has an important "real" job in the outside world and he is a little concerned that his boss might read this book. (As if his boss reads anything but *Robb Report* and *Yachting Magazine!*) Anyway, C.B. would like to remain as anonymous as possible just in case he decides to run for president someday or join a country club. He's married to Ida and they have two kids, Sherman and Violet.

Neither my dad nor my brother would be caught dead working in pajamas. My dad now works from home and he still puts on a suit to "go to work" in his home office. Casual Friday for C.B. means "wild" striped trouser socks and jeans that can only be dry-cleaned.

# INTRODUCTION

I remember the first time my dad told me to get a job. I was about ten years old and I was begging him to buy me something and his response was, "Go get a job and make your own money if you want that."

You know what? He should have been more careful. I'll never say that to my kids, because I hated school so much that I would have gladly dropped out right then. I didn't need much. I had a roof over my head. My parents fed and clothed me. In my ten-year-old mind I thought all I needed was enough money to buy some gum and maybe some badass rainbow suspenders. I know that's what my kids think too. They get a hundred bucks from Grandma for Christmas and they think they can live on that for a year.

To a kid, jobs look like fun. I know I thought the idea of working in an office sounded cool. I wanted to be just like the three working girls in the movie *9 to 5*. Except the part where Jane Fonda was forced to find a job because her husband abandoned her. And the part where Lily Tomlin tried to kill their tyrannical boss by accidentally dumping rat poison into his coffee. And the part where Dolly Parton was sexually harassed. Hang on, maybe this movie wasn't appropriate for kids? Nice job letting me see it, Mom and Dad.

Of course I thought a job looked great! I didn't know yet about brown-nosing jerks who take the credit for all the work you do. I didn't understand office politics. I didn't realize having a job meant I had to show up every day, all day, even when I didn't really feel like it. I thought that once I had enough money, I could just quit for a while and come back when I ran out of cash.

The first job I applied for was to work at the local movie theater. It was a small, one-screen operation run by a guy who none of the moms in town trusted. They let us go to the movies, but always with a stern warning: "Do not talk to that guy. Always go to the bathroom in groups. Make sure you wait outside to be picked up, I don't care if there's snow on the ground." You would think that if our moms were so concerned about the dude, they might actually go to the movies with us. Apparently the idea of sitting through *Sixteen Candles* was just too much for them. They'd rather send us off with a lecture and a prayer that we didn't get molested in the ladies' room.

I was in sixth grade and I liked the idea of getting paid to eat popcorn and watch movies all weekend, because I thought that's what you did when you worked at a movie theater. After watching *Ghostbusters* for probably the eight-ieth time, I stopped by the owner's office on my way out the door and asked for an application.

"How old are you?" he asked.

"Twelve," I said.

He said, "State law won't let me hire someone so young, but you could work here for free. Would you like that? You can have a large popcorn every shift you work."

The large popcorn *was* enticing, but I really wanted dollars too. "I don't think my dad would let me work for free," I said.

"He doesn't need to know," the man replied, wagging his bushy eyebrows. "I can keep secrets. Can you?"

It was suddenly very apparent to me why this guy creeped out the moms. I got the hell out of there as fast as I could.

Instead of working for the child molester for free at the movie theater, I accepted a job offer from my neighbor. She offered to pay me fifty cents to stay with her napping baby while she ran to pick up her older child from school. I was terrible at this job. My only duty was to sit on the couch and watch TV until the mother returned. If a fire broke out spontaneously or an intruder kicked in the front door, I was expected to rescue the sleeping baby and run for help. That's it. But I was baby crazy. I loved playing with babies. But babies can't play with you when they're asleep. So about five minutes into my thirty-minute job, I'd imagine a sound.

"What was that? Was that Baby Egberta stirring? Is she wet? Is she hungry?"

Because I was a damn good babysitter, I couldn't ignore those (imaginary) sounds. What if they were real? So I'd sneak up the stairs and poke my head into Egberta's room. From the doorway all seemed fine, but I didn't get paid the big bucks of two quarters to take any chances. I'd tiptoe a bit farther into the room all stealthy-like, but in my haste to ascertain the wellness of my charge, I would carelessly overlook a noisy toy discarded on the carpet. Sure enough, I'd manage to hit that squeaky/shrilly/barking toy square on, immediately waking the baby.

"WAHHHHHHHHH!" Egberta would immediately scream.

What could I do? She was an unhappy baby at that point. My job was to make her happy and so I'd drag her out of her crib and put her on the floor where we could play for the next twenty-five minutes before her mother and brother returned home.

At twelve, I didn't understand the look on Egberta's mother's face when she'd come home and find Egberta fully awake and ready to be entertained for the next several hours. I would wonder, "Why does Egberta's mom look so disappointed to see her? She's so cute, the way she climbs on everything and pulls all the books off shelves and tips over lamps and sticks random forks into outlets, almost electrocuting herself on the daily. I can't wait to be a mom! It will be so much fun to play with my kids all day long."

Yeah, I really thought that. At twelve I didn't think motherhood was anything but dressing up babies in adorable clothing, reading books, and playing blocks all day. That's probably why I made such a good babysitter. Sure, I woke up the babies, but at least I didn't neglect them. You'd never find Jenni Mann, Babysitter, on the phone with her friends while the kids drank cleaning fluid or sat mindlessly in front of a television.

I spent many of my weekends babysitting. I had no desire to flip burgers or work retail. When I went off to college, I tried to find jobs that would pay me to do what I loved: writing. And then I graduated and realized that writing jobs were tough to find. So, I started down a long road of several McJobs (thank you, Douglas Coupland, for teaching me that terrific word to describe my career path), hoping that one of them—any of them—could turn into a career, but never giving up hope that maybe someday I'd be a writer.

THE EARLY YEARS

# CHAPTER 1

## HOW I BECAME THE RICHEST LOSER IN JUNIOR HIGH AND THE ENVY OF ALL THE NEIGHBORHOOD SOCCER MOMS

I GOT my first real job in the seventh grade. I'd just started junior high and I had my first pair of Guess jeans and more neon bling than days to wear it all.

Even though I had such a strong fashion sense, I didn't have much of a life in seventh grade. Not that anyone did, but you know what I mean. It was the nineteen eighties, so most of my friends spent their weekends hanging out at the mall or going to movies or the roller rink. I wanted to go every weekend but my parents complained about the expense. I have no idea how much it cost, maybe a couple of bucks, but it "added up," as they liked to tell me. I could have paid for myself, but I didn't have the dough. I could earn an allowance, but unfortunately in my house, allowance was earned by cleaning and getting good grades. I failed my mother's weekly white glove test because I didn't dust *behind* the books on my shelves and I left footprints in my vacuum tracks. I was a C student at best, and even though I would often argue that someone has to be average to make the smart kids feel superior, my parents were not in the business of rewarding mediocrity. Thus, it seemed like I was always running in the red.

I could blame my lack of social life on limited funds but the truth was I was rarely invited. I was not a popular kid, nor was I a real outgoing kid. So most weekends were spent on the couch, nestled between my parents, watching whatever was on the three channels we had to choose from back then. (You youngsters have no idea how good you have it now! If my kids scroll through two hundred and fifty channels and complain one more time that there's nothing to watch I will force them to watch *Laurel & Hardy* VHS tapes so they will understand my pain.)

We'd moved to a new neighborhood that summer and many of our neighbors had come over to introduce themselves. After the introductions, there was always some good gossip to be shared too. Since I had no life, I found myself at the kitchen table drinking tea with my mom and getting the scoop from some nosybody about who was sleeping with who, and who didn't cut their yard nice enough, and who let their dog shit in your yard, and then it would always come around to "You know you live across the street from The Quints, right? At least we *think* they live there. They never come outside."

The Quints were famous in our small town. They were the only set of quintuplets born in the state or something like that. They'd been on the news when they were born and then they disappeared into their home, never to be seen again!

"How old are they?" I asked, hoping they were close to my age.

"Maybe three?" the busybody said.

"Oh. Little," I replied.

"Yes, I saw them once last winter. All bundled up in

coats and snow pants. They were outside for about five minutes having photos taken. So strange!"

"I don't think that sounds very strange," my mom said. "Don't you remember getting kids ready to play out in the snow? It took so much work and then one always needed to go to the bathroom as soon as you got out there. I can't imagine trying to do that with five kids! I probably wouldn't leave my house that much either."

"Hmm," the busybody said. "I still think it's strange. They're so unfriendly."

"Maybe they're just private," Mom said.

A few weeks later I was walking home from the bus stop when I saw a small, dark-haired woman standing at the end of my driveway. She watched me approach but didn't move or speak. She just stared at me.

When I got closer I realized she was a woman I'd never seen before. "Hello?" I said. "Can I help you?"

"You live here, right?" She jerked her head toward my house.

"Yes," I said, glancing at the house.

"How old are you? Thirteen?"

"Almost."

"I've been watching you."

"You have?" I asked. I didn't know if I should be scared or proud that I had a stalker.

"What's your name?" she asked.

"Jenni," I said. God, I was stupid! The woman said she'd been watching me and I was still willing to give up my name. I clearly wanted to be kidnapped!

"You're a good kid?"

Was that a question? "Um, yeah, I guess."

"I watch you."

"Yeah, you said that."

"You don't have boys coming and going. You don't do stupid stuff. No parties or anything."

"Yeah, because I'm *twelve*," I said.

"You seem normal," she said.

"Okay."

"I want you to work for me," she said, nodding.

I frowned. "I'm too young to work. I already tried to get a job at the movie theater and they said I had to be sixteen."

"Yeah, well, I like that you're young. You'll actually do what you're told and you won't be distracted by the dumb shit teenagers are distracted by."

I was startled to hear her swear. My parents never cussed and neither did their friends, at least not in front of me. I felt like a grown-up. The woman seemed kind of nuts, but also intriguing. "I'm sorry, who are you exactly?"

The woman finally smiled. "You really don't know who I am?"

"No, should I?" Was she famous or something? "I'm Marci. I live across the street. I'm the mother of 'The Quints.'" She made air quotes. "Well, the quints *and* Sally. They always forget Sally. She was first, you know."

"The quints?" I asked, trying to pretend like that was the first I'd heard of the miracle babies across the street who were being held prisoners in their own home.

"Come on, this whole neighborhood loves to talk shit about me and my kids. I can only imagine what you've heard. My sister lives up the street and her next-door neighbor told her that she heard my kids have some kind of allergy to the sun and so they only come outside and play at night. Can you believe that? People are so stupid."

I didn't know what to say, because I'd heard the same rumor and I'd totally believed it.

"Here's the deal. When the quints were born it made

the news. We got all kinds of gifts and stuff, but we also got a lot of crackpots who came out of the woodwork. Like, nutso people who wanted to steal my kids. Yes, it's difficult to leave the house with six kids—including Sally—but it's nearly impossible when you're terrified some nutjob is going to try and steal one or two of them when you're not looking. So, we stayed inside. A lot. And really, who was I going to socialize with? Betsy from next door who tells everyone that I'm a weirdo? You know she's a drunk, right? Check her garbage bins next week. You'll see. And there's Margo who lives behind me. She's always doing fundraisers and shit for the town. She rebuilt the library or something like that. She's always like, 'Marci, come to this gala I'm hosting.' What she doesn't say is, 'You need to squeeze your fat ass into a cocktail dress and drop two hundred bucks so I can tell everyone you're the mother of the quints and they can stare at you.'"

I stared dumbly. I found Marci fascinating. She literally had no fucks to give (and her ass was not fat at all). My mom was one of those moms who always worried what the neighbors would think. She kept our house immaculate and dressed us up. She didn't gossip or judge people. She just kept in her lane and didn't have strong opinions about much. I loved my mom, but I *really* liked Marci. "I'm sorry, what is the job?" I asked.

"I want you to be my babysitter," Marci said. "I have two full-time nannies, but both of them have Saturdays off. After all of these kids, my husband and I need to rekindle our relationship—y'know what I mean?" (I did not.) "And so we've decided that every Saturday night we're going to go on a date."

"You're going to date your husband?" I asked, confused.

Why would you date someone you're already married to? It made no sense to me.

"Yeah! We have to go somewhere nice or do something fun. No talking about kids or work or money or whatever. Just connecting with one another. Does that make sense?"

"Umm, kinda," I said. My parents did not date. They went to couples' events at our church or to parent-teacher conferences. Once they went on a vacation without me and my younger brother, C.B., and I never forgave them.

"Anyway, it doesn't matter why we're doing it, it matters that it's happening. But we need a babysitter. I've been watching you and it doesn't look like you've got much going on," Marci said.

*Thank you??*

She continued, "Most Saturday nights you're here. Lights are out by ten—that's your room at the front of the house, right?"

I nodded. *What the hell??*

"Great, so every Saturday night we need you. Five till ten-ish. Kids will be bathed and I'll leave something easy for you to feed them. Just stuff you can nuke. Feed them, play with them till seven and then the rest of the night is yours. We have cable and a fully stocked pantry. You can call your friends, but absolutely no visitors. Got it?"

"Got it," I said.

"You like kids, right?" Marci asked, suddenly concerned.

I nodded. "I do, actually. They're fun to play with."

"All right. Great. What do you charge?"

"For babysitting?" I asked.

"Yeah. Of course."

I racked my brain. This would be a lot different from

sitting with the sleeping Egberta while her mother ran to the grocery store for half an hour. This was going to be the quints—and Sally—and they'd be awake and stuff, so I said, "Two dollars an hour?" I bit my lip, hoping I wasn't reaching too high. Marci laughed. "Two dollars?" I squirmed a bit. I almost said a buck fifty, but then I decided to hold firm. Two dollars for six kids seemed fair, so I nodded.

Marci frowned. "Here's the thing, Jenni, you're in a unique position. I want you. No, I *need* you. Do not sell yourself short. Ask for the moon. The worst I can say is no."

I licked my dry lips. "Three dollars an hour?"

"Come on, Jenni! Think about it, if you're only worth three bucks an hour, then why the hell do I want you with my kids? Have some pride. Have some self-worth! How does ten dollars an hour sound?" *Like I just won the lottery!* "Good," I squeaked.

"Good," Marci said, nodding. "Now, listen carefully. Word's going to get out that you're my sitter now. It's going to get out mostly because I'm going to tell Margo and that shit's gonna spread like wildfire. They're going to all start calling you—the neighborhood hens—and ask you to sit for their kids. And that's great. I hope you get a lot of business from this. But! Do not take less than ten bucks an hour from any of them. I don't care if it's one sleeping baby or four little nightmares who swing from the chandelier. It's minimum ten bucks an hour. Got it? You're worth it. Also, some of them might even try to book you for a Saturday. You can never, ever, *ever* give up your Saturday to anyone else. Saturdays are mine. I own Saturdays. Always. Count on it. I don't care if they offer you fifteen bucks an hour, I'm your Saturday job. They can give you fifteen on Fridays. Do we have an understanding?"

I nodded. "Of course," I said, because really, who else was going to pay me ten dollars an hour to babysit?

But Marci knew what she was talking about. That night I received a phone call from Betsy, the alleged drunk.

"You don't know me, but I'm looking for a babysitter and you've come highly recommended," she said.

"By who?" I asked.

"Everyone," she replied. "I need a sitter for this Saturday night. I pay twelve dollars an hour."

"I'm sorry, I already have a job for Saturday," I said.

"Cancel it," she said. "I'm paying twelve dollars an hour."

It was just like Marci predicted! "No, I'm sorry, I can't. But I can do Friday," I said.

The woman sighed heavily. "Fine, Friday. But I only pay eight on Fridays."

Eight was still a shit ton of money, but Marci's words haunted me. "No, I'm sorry, my rate is ten dollars an hour," I said.

"Are you really the preferred babysitter for the quints?"

"And their sister, Sally," I said. "Don't forget Sally."

"Marci's really paying you ten bucks an hour?" Betsy said.

"That's my starting rate."

"This is ridiculous," Betsy said. "I did not believe Margo when she told me. Marci doesn't let anyone near those kids. How did you get the job?"

"I don't know," I said truthfully. "We just talked for a bit and she offered it to me."

"Well, what's your experience?"

"Um, not a lot. This will be my first real babysitting job where the kids are awake and I'm expected to do stuff with them."

"Oh, this is insanity! Why did she choose you? What is so great about you?" Betsy seethed. "She's just doing this to mess with the rest of us. You know that, right?"

"I don't know anything about that," I said.

"Have you even seen the kids? What are they like? I bet they're wild."

"I haven't met them yet," I said. "But I'm not worried. They sound fine."

"Your parents are fine with you babysitting that many kids?"

"It wasn't even something we discussed," I said.

"You're very young!"

"Marci said that's one of things she likes about me."

"I can't even believe this! Fine. If Marci thinks you can take care of her six kids, then surely you can handle my two. Come on Friday night."

"And you'll pay ten dollars an hour?" I asked.

"Yes, yes."

I hung up the phone and it immediately rang again. "Hello?"

"Is this Marci's babysitter?"

It went on like that for days. I ended up babysitting all the time, sometimes five or six nights a week. I didn't have much of a social life over the next few years, but I could afford to go to the roller rink on Saturday night if I didn't have the quints and Sally to babysit.

Some Saturdays Marci and Paul would be too exhausted for date night, so they'd send one of the kids over with a twenty and a note:

*GO OUT WITH YOUR FRIENDS. DON'T TAKE ANOTHER JOB. MARCI.*

Marci's sister would always test me on those nights. She'd beg me to come over and she'd promise not to tell Marci, but I would never go. It was too important to me to keep Marci happy. She was a great boss and I really loved taking care of the quints and Sally. Besides valuing the work Marci gave me, I really valued the time she spent with me too. When you're thirteen it's hard to talk to your parents about the shit that's going on in your life, but you need an adult who can listen and guide you. Marci was that person. A lot of times when Marci would get home, she'd sit up and talk to me about my life. She was a huge influence on me. Marci taught me about loyalty, how to swear properly, how to parent without fucks, how to deal with bitchy neighbors, how to date your husband, and how to value yourself.

I remember sitting at the kitchen counter and thinking how I wanted to be Marci when I grew up—just with fewer kids. Because the quints and Sally were a lot of fun, but they were also a shit ton of work.

## CHAPTER 2

### THAT AWKWARD MOMENT WHEN YOUR COLLEGE ADVISOR TELLS YOU TO LOSE YOUR DREAMS AND MAJOR IN YOUR MRS.

WHEN I WENT off to college in 1990, I thought I'd be a schoolteacher. My mom and dad had sat me down in June to talk about life goals and budgets and other grown-up shit. Once they told me that I couldn't live in their basement and collect cats for the rest of my life, we decided I should be a schoolteacher. It made sense for me. My whole work experience up until that point was babysitting and I was good at it. I liked *some* kids, and the pro of summers off outweighed the cons of sticky, smelly children. I figured I could turn my skill set into a career if I majored in elementary education. I wasn't thrilled with the idea, but I didn't hate it either.

It only took about three days for me to realize that teaching was not the same as babysitting. Not even close. I had to actually know some shit and then I had to teach it to kids! Wiggly, giggly, snotty kids. I had to design lesson plans and read textbooks with names like *The Psychology of the Gifted Child* and *The Psychology of the Not-So-Gifted Child*. What I really liked about elementary education I realized was designing those huge bulletin boards in the hallways of the school and reading books out loud during snack time. Other than that, being a teacher seemed awful to me. Way too much work was involved and it was a giant responsibility. I was not prepared to really mold future generations—I could barely figure out my own life!

So at the end of my first week of college, I changed my major to English. I was surprised I didn't choose English from the beginning. I'd been writing stories since I was five. As soon as I could form letters, I wrote down the stories inside my head. Before you think I'm going to go down the whole *I was some kind of a prodigy and an ah-may-zing writer at five years old* path, just wait. Remember: this is *me* we're talking about here. I've never done jack shit on an *ah-may-zing* level.

No, my stories were quite familiar, actually. A little *too* familiar. I wrote about a little country mouse who visits his family in the big city. He has a terrible experience and several brushes with death. He finally decides the city is too wild and he's a simple country mouse who likes the peace and quiet and safety of the country better. Do you think you've heard that story before? That's because Aesop wrote it. Yeah, it's one of Aesop's Fables.

How about this adorable Jenni Original: a horribly deformed young man lives in his family's basement and every day a beautiful girl comes to tutor him and they fall in love despite his abnormalities. (Although, keep in mind, I was five at the time. So it was probably just: Once there was an ugly man with lumps on him who fell in love with a beautiful girl who was his teacher. She loved him back, even though he was ugly and lumpy and she was beautiful. The End.)

When my mother read that one, she gasped. She was

positive she was in the presence of greatness. "Jenni just wrote the story of *The Elephant Man!*" she told my father.

"What do you mean?" he asked.

"Look! She wrote a story and it's basically *The Elephant Man!* How does she come up with this stuff? Last week she wrote one of *Aesop's Fables*. I've never read those to her. They're *sooo* boring. She must be *gifted!*"

"Or she saw it on your soap opera. Weren't you just telling me the other day that Rock was burned in an oil rig explosion or something?"

"His name is Stone and no, it was a mining accident. It was crazy. He was just mining for coal, as he does most weekends since it's his hobby, and suddenly BOOM! Investigators believe it was a buildup of methane."

"Yeah, okay, *anyway*...Stone didn't die though, right?"

"No. He's alive, but just barely. The doctors are pretty sure his face is maimed underneath all the bandages. He was burned pretty bad. Plus, he forgot how to speak and read and write and so his nurse, Nicolletta, has been teaching him."

"And there it is. Yeah, our daughter is not a genius. This story isn't so much *The Elephant Man* as it is *Hope and Heartbreak Through Time*."

"That's not the name of my soap!"

"You know what I mean."

I'm going to go with my dad on this one. I don't remember anyone reading me *Aesop's Fables*, but I do remember playing in the family room while my mother watched one soap opera after another.

I'm not saying my mother was a layabout who ate bonbons all day while she watched her "stories." It was the seventies, so the TV was always on as constant background noise while she did her housework. She was always vacuuming (I swear, the most vivid memory I have of my whole childhood is my mother either vacuuming, putting away the vacuum, or the vacuum sitting in the middle of the front hall waiting to be used and/or put away—I think that's why I despise vacuuming to this day) or ironing my dad's undershirts. (Yeah, she really did that. She was a total slacker, though, because *her* mother ironed sheets, which my mother refused to do. In that same tradition, I refuse to buy anything that requires ironing. My grandmother is disgusted by the both of us.)

After I declared my new major, I had to meet with an advisor in the English department named Eudora to talk about my new career path. Eudora suggested I still get a degree in education and English and then I could teach high school.

"But I don't want to teach. Kids kind of suck, especially ones who aren't related to you," I said. "I want to be a writer."

Her face was so kind and gentle when she unloaded the cold, hard truth on me. "Do you know any writers, Jen?" she asked.

I thought about it. "No, not really."

"It's an incredibly tough business to break into," she said. "That's why I thought education would be good for you. Give you something to fall back on." The "when it doesn't work out" part was silent, but it was implied.

"I like hanging out with kids, but I don't think I like teaching them," I said, wrinkling my nose at the thought of grading papers.

"What about college students?" Eudora suggested. "You could get your master's and then you could be a professor?"

That sounded a bit better to me. "Yeah, maybe," I said noncommittally, because I was already looking down the barrel of four years of schooling and she was talking about tacking on even more!

"What about journalism?" she suggested.

"Hmm, I don't know. You have to write the truth, right?"

Eudora laughed. "Yes, newspapers like to print the truth," she said. "How about technical writing?"

"What's that?" I asked.

"Well, it's writing everything that you read throughout the day. Instruction manuals, guides, contracts, catalogs, that sort of thing."

"Hmm." I hadn't told my parents yet that I had changed majors and I knew they weren't going to be happy with me, especially if I called them up and said, "Surprise! I'm majoring in creative writing! I'll never get a job and I'll probably always live in your basement!" Maybe if I told them I was thinking about getting a technical writing job after graduation, they wouldn't be so upset. Technical writer sounded like a writer who had her shit together. "Yeah, I think I like that. I mean, someone has to write lather, rinse, repeat, right?"

"Well, that's been done, so you'd do something else," Eudora said, frowning.

"Jeez, so serious, Eudora!" I said.

She laughed, but just barely.

A few weeks into my new major Eudora stopped me after class one day. "Jen, there's a job opening at *The Black & Gold*," she said. "I was thinking you should apply."

*The Black & Gold* was the alumni magazine. For a freshman English major, it was a big deal just to be asked to apply. "Really? You think so?" I asked.

Eudora nodded. "Yes, I think you'd do great there. Your voice would be a nice change."

I sent over my resume to the editor and some samples of my work. I say it was an honor, but maybe no one else applied because somehow I got the job and for the first time I was earning money for writing!

That made the conversation with my parents so much easier. My dad had this thing where he would call me every Saturday morning at the ass crack of dawn. He told me he was paying a fortune for my education and he wanted me to make sure I was getting the full experience and not sleeping through any of it. I really think he did it because he knew I was out drinking on Friday night and he just wanted to be an asshole. I tried to turn off the ringer once, but I immediately found my credit card canceled. I never pulled that shit again. So when my phone rang that Saturday morning at six, I was ready.

After the usual "nothings" and "not muches," I finally got around to saying, "Soooo, I changed my major."

"What? You did?" Mom said. I could practically hear her clutch her pearls.

"Why?" Dad asked.

"I'm not cut out for teaching," I said. "Too many kids."

"You love kids, Jenni," Mom said.

"Yeah, but not enough to spend all day with them, you know? Also, there was a lot of stuff I had to do. Lesson plans and psychology tests and it sounded like a nightmare."

"Okay," Dad said. "So what did you change your major to?"

"English."

"English?" Dad said. "What are you going to do with an English degree?"

"My advisor says I can be a technical writer."

"What's that?" Mom asked.

"It's a real job you can get," I said.

"Does it pay well?" Dad asked.

"Um, does teaching?" I replied. "I'm not sure what you're so worried about here."

"I'm worried that you won't be able to afford your lifestyle," Dad said. "I have no intention of supporting you your whole life."

"Well, don't worry, because I already have a job that's paying me to write."

"You do?" Mom asked.

"Yeah, I'm writing for *The Black & Gold*," I said.

"We get that magazine!" Mom said.

"Of course you do, you're alumni."

"I haven't seen your name in there," Dad said.

"I have the cover story of the next issue," I said. "I mean, don't start redecorating my room yet or anything, but I'm on my way!"

"Of course you are!" Mom gushed.

"Huh," Dad said, slightly impressed, but I could tell he was still thinking about me living in his basement in twenty years.

"*The Black & Gold* is just the first step toward my writing career," I assured my parents. "It's going to be great!"

And it was until I met Randall.

It was the beginning of my sophomore year when I received a request for a meeting with Randall. I'd heard rumors about him, but we'd never met. Randall was the head of the English department. The previous year he was on sabbatical writing his Great American Novel but he was back and ready to take over his duties from Eudora. I'd really enjoyed having Eudora as my advisor and I wanted to stay with her, but I was told that Randall advised all the creative writing majors and so I'd have to switch to him.

I showed up for my appointment and found him in his office, going through my writing samples. "Where's your poetry?" he asked curtly. No greeting, no handshake, just right to my work—or lack thereof.

"Um, I don't really write poetry," I said. "I didn't take a poetry class last year, so unless I have to write it for a class, I don't write poems."

"How can you call yourself a creative writing major and not write poetry?" he demanded, rubbing his eyes like I was exhausting him.

I shrugged. "I didn't know I had to," I said.

"Well, what are you working on right now?" he asked.

"Mostly schoolwork. I want to take playwriting next semester, so I've started brainstorming some one-act ideas."

"Playwriting?" he scoffed. "*That's* writing?"

I frowned. This was not how my meetings with Eudora went. She was always encouraging me with my writing. She never mentioned poetry, and it was her idea to write a one-act play. "Eudora says that any writing is writing. It's all creative and necessary and it's worthwhile."

"Of course Eudora would say that. She coddles you people," Randall sneered. "She's the one who got you the job writing for *The Black & Gold*, right?"

"Yes," I said proudly. "It's been great for me. I can make some money and I'll have some professional samples when I graduate and apply to magazines and stuff."

"Ha! No one of consequence is going to care about your time at *The Black & Gold*. No one reads it, not even the dean."

"It has a pretty large circulation," I said.

"Yes, because as soon as you graduate you're put on the mailing list whether you want it or not. I guarantee half those magazines are going to dead people."

"I was thinking about applying for the newspaper," I said, hoping he'd like that idea better. I was trying to please the man, but nothing was working.

"I'm the advisor to the newspaper," Randall said. "There's no place for you there. You might as well stay at *The Black & Gold*. Are you writing any fiction?"

"Um, no, not right now. I don't really have the time."

"Well, you need to make the time if you want to succeed, Jen. Look at me, I took a whole year off to write my book."

I tried not to roll my eyes, because did he really think I had an entire year to dedicate to writing a book? "Yes, I know. How is it doing?" I asked.

"It's in the campus bookstore. You should get a copy."

"I'll look for it," I said, but I had no desire to get a copy of his shitty fifty-dollar book. Later on he would force me to buy it when he assigned it to our class to read the following semester.

"Why don't you have education as your backup?" he asked.

I shrugged again. "I don't really want to teach and if I get a degree in education, I'll feel like I should use it."

"But you think you're going to use your creative writing degree?"

"Yeah, I think so," I said. "Eudora thinks I can do technical writing or marketing. I'm kind of witty. I mean, I did win the writing scholarship." My college was very small and there was only one writing scholarship, so I didn't need to say anything more.

"I wasn't on the judging committee for your year. I was already on sabbatical. If your submission was anything like these samples or what I've read in *The Black & Gold*, I can tell you, you would not have made the cut. Not even close."

And then he literally drew a giant black X through the page in front of him.

I didn't know what to say. I'd never been a very confident young adult, but one of the few areas where I really believed in myself was my writing ability. My high school English teacher had encouraged me, and Eudora had helped me find avenues that actually resulted in money. Up until that point I hadn't had one person criticize my work the way Randall was. Sure, I'd been critiqued, but it was always given in such a way that I knew what I needed to improve or change or fix or just own as my voice. Randall was drawing big black lines wildly and not offering any sort of constructive feedback that I could use. I had no idea what I'd done to deserve his disgust.

"Are we done here?" I asked.

"Yes, but we're going to be meeting once a week to go over your work," Randall said.

"Are we really going to go over it or are you just going to tell me it sucks?" I asked.

Randall glared, but didn't argue with me.

If I thought I could change my major again, I would have done it that day. Randall was such a horrible human being and the thought of spending the next three years with him made me both angry and sad all at the same time. But I had to stay. There was nothing else I wanted to do with my life. I'd just have to put up with Randall and try to figure out a way to please him.

That was easier said than done. I tried so hard to do what he wanted, but nothing was good enough for him. And it wasn't just my work he didn't like. It was personal. He went out of his way to let me know how much I sucked. He kissed the asses of his class pets and tried to publicly humiliate me. And I let him.

I let Randall beat me down over the next three years. I let him belittle my job at *The Black & Gold*. I let him scoff when my one-act play was one of the few chosen to be produced. And then there was the day he read my poem out loud to the class. The poems were anonymous and so he had no idea it was mine. He went on and on about how my poem was full of sexual overtones. "That smell the narrator is railing against is the smell of post-coital bodies," he said. "The smell of bodies intertwined after a heated and powerful lovemaking session."

My poem had been written at dinner the night before on a napkin in the cafeteria. It was about the nasty smelling food they were serving us. "Do you like that poem, Randall?" I asked.

"I do. It has so much raw sexual energy coursing through it."

"I wrote it," I said. "It's about Meatloaf Monday," I said.

That didn't go over well. If Randall already didn't like me, embarrassing him in front of the class didn't help.

A few weeks later I was sitting in his office for our final meeting before graduation. I was almost done with the man. One more conversation and then I could be rid of him forever. He was still smarting from poetry class, so I knew the meeting would be a rough one.

"Do you have any job leads?" he asked, his eyes boring into me.

"Um, kind of," I said. "Ron, my editor at *The Black & Gold*, has written me a letter of recommendation that I've sent out with my resume. I have an interview with *Produce Manager Magazine* next month."

"*Produce Manager Magazine*?"

"Yeah, it's a trade publication aimed at produce

managers around the country. I'd be the editor, which is kind of cool."

"Fascinating," Randall mocked. "Seriously, Jen, what are you going to do? You graduate in a week and you still don't have a job? You have one interview with some random publication that no one cares about and that's it?"

"My parents said I can come home and stay with them for a bit while I look."

"Of course they did." He rolled his eyes. "No wonder you're not worried. Your daddy will just add you to his payroll."

"Yeah, maybe," I said. "Maybe I can use the free time to finally write something."

"You should have focused on getting married," Randall said.

"Excuse me?"

"You're never going to use your degree. No one is going to buy a want ad from you, let alone a book. You have no talent. What you need is a husband. You should have gotten a husband. You wasted your opportunity."

My mouth fell open. It was nineteen fucking ninety-four and an older male authority figure was dropping this shit on me like it was nineteen forty-four. I didn't know what offended me more—the fact that he said my writing sucked, or that he told me I needed a man to take care of me and that at twenty-two I was already a damaged old maid with limited prospects.

I'd had enough of Randall. I didn't need to hear him any more. I had so much rage coursing through my body at that point. Rage at Randall, rage at myself for letting him treat me so poorly, fear that maybe he was right, anger with myself for the self-doubt I was feeling. You name it, I was pissed at it. I had to go. I couldn't sit there another minute and listen to his fucking demeaning and demoralizing speeches. I stood up, picked up my book bag and walked to the door. I'd like to tell you that I told off Randall that day. That I unleashed a scathing and withering diatribe that reduced him to a puddle of tears. But I didn't. I didn't have the courage. Instead, I scurried out of his office, mere seconds from crying, and I muttered under my breath like a witch cursing an old man who stole her youth. "Just you wait, Randall. Some day I'll send you my book and I'll sign it 'Dear Randall—What does this book smell like? Sex? No, it smells like success, you fucker.'"

# CHAPTER 3

## NEPOTISM AND POCKET PROTECTORS: MY FIRST REAL JOB

I GRADUATED from college in 1995 and my parents' graduation gift to me was a fancy leather briefcase from the Coach outlet and a ream of paper for making copies of my resume. I immediately began looking for a job. But I didn't want a McJob, I wanted a "career." I wasn't going to take just any old job to pay my bills. I had busted my ass for the past four (and a half) years and now I wanted to use my newfound skills in a high-paying, high-profile job. I wanted to work somewhere I felt valued and respected! I wanted to find a place where I could move up the corporate ladder and give them the best twenty-five years of my life! Meanwhile, I'd attended a college where I could barely get a telephone jack in my room, let alone cable television. So it was no surprise that for the past four (and a half) years, I'd missed out on every bit of news regarding the "worst economy for graduates" since who knows when. I did know we were in a war, but that was only because my professors talked about it occasionally in my classes. When you're an English major you know all about the politics of Verona, but not so much about D.C.

After a few months of sending out resumes (on pink paper so it would stand out from the masses—thank you to my liberal arts college for providing me with *that* helpful tidbit) to companies that I wanted to work for, I realized that my credit card bill was due and I'd better find a job quick. That's when I started sending out resumes to companies that didn't even advertise an opening. I was so sure my pink resume would make such an impression on my dream company that they would just *create* a job for me.

After a string of nos, my dad suggested I apply for a job at QuikTrip. In case you don't know, QuikTrip, aka QT, is a gas station with about a thousand fountain drinks and lottery tickets, but mostly it sells gas. My dad let me know that QT was looking for overnight managers and the job required a college education.

"Um...what? Wait, Dad, but don't you get shot working the overnight shift in gas stations? Plus, you just dropped fifty thousand on my education. Surely I'm overqualified to run a cash register and sell cigarettes?"

"They pay forty thousand a year," he said, barely looking up from the want ads he was scouring for me. "Plus benefits. I bet you even get a discount on the fountain drinks."

"Dad, I have a degree in creative writing. I am going to write the definitive novel of my generation!"

"Well, that's perfect. You'll have plenty of time to write it during your downtime on the overnight shift at QT, don't you think?"

"Dad! What do you want me to do? Scribble notes on the backs of receipts? I can't write my book under those conditions!" (Little did I know that almost twenty-five years later I would be scribbling notes for *this* book on the backs of receipts while dodging balls at soccer practice or sitting poolside during semi-private swim lessons. It's amazing the "conditions" I can work under now!)

"You'd be surprised what you can accomplish if you put your mind to it."

"I know. In fact, I've been thinking. I could go to law school!"

"Not with your grades."

Ugh. He was right. There wasn't a law school in the country that would take someone with my GPA. "Okay! I will find something, but I will *not* work in a gas station!"

"Whatever, but I canceled your AmEx today."

"*Daaaad,* I need that card. I need a new suit for job interviews!"

"QT has a uniform. That could cut down your expenses a lot."

"You're killing me, Dad."

"Uh huh. Here's the number to call."

I looked at the ad he'd circled and I started hyperventilating a little bit thinking about the pros and cons of this job.

CONS:

• Overnight shift. Seriously? I loved my sleep and I was not a good day sleeper, so unless there was a place to nap in the back, I didn't see how I could possibly make it through a shift.

• Uniform. I was not a fashion diva in any sense, but even I drew the line at the QT uniform. It was not flattering on anyone.

• I would always smell like gasoline. How was I going to attract a husband when I smelled like gas?

• I could get shot. Gas stations got robbed all the time. I was not prepared to take a bullet for QT. Surely that shit was insured. I would just hand over the cash drawer and tell the robber to help himself to some lottery tickets and a slushee on his way out the door.

PROS:

• $40,000 per year. *Produce Manager Magazine* didn't even offer me half of that.

• Free Cokes. Dad was wrong about the discount; they were actually free. But QT was going to lose money on me, because I would need to drink a shit ton of cold, caffeinated beverages to stay awake all night.

• $40,000 per year.

• Downtime to write my novel. As if that was going to happen. For starters, in order to write my book I needed absolute silence, a comfy chair, a desk with a computer, a notepad and freshly sharpened pencils—more for the smell than for their actual usefulness since I'd be typing---and no gasoline fumes making me high.

• $40,000 per year.

QuikTrip and its forty grand was looking more attractive by the minute, but that uniform though. My ass was not made for tan polyester.

I was desperate. I needed a job fast. So I did what most suburban middle class white kids do: I appealed to my family members to pull some strings and get me a job—any job—at their company.

Since my dad was self-employed and not hiring, I had to venture deep into the outer realms of my blood ties. My uncle was a church minister, so that was never going to work. His wife was a teacher, and since I didn't get my fall-back education degree I couldn't appeal to her. I had to branch out even farther on the family tree. That's where I found my great uncle Monty. He looked like an excellent soft target. He worked at a local engineering firm (so I could still live at home, much to my mother's delight and my father's dismay) and he was on the lifer career track (which meant he was a yes man). He'd put in the necessary years with the firm that he had a few strings to pull to get his third-favorite great-niece an entry-level job so she wouldn't have to sell corn dogs and scratch-offs. Monty was perfect. He was a company man through and through. Every morning when he got dressed for work, the last touch was the tie tack the company had given him for fifteen years of service or some such bullshit.

I called up Uncle Monty and had to remind him who I was. "Hi, Uncle Monty, it's Jen!"

"Who?"

"Jen Mann, your great-niece."

"Who?"

"Jennnn...Maaannnnn," I said slowly and loudly, because I thought maybe he was hard of hearing. He was pretty old.

"Jen Mann? Is this Ruby's daughter?"

"No, Uncle Monty, I'm Karen's daughter, not Ruby's."

"Karen, huh? I know Ruby, but I don't know Karen."

"Ruby's my aunt. She's Karen's sister? You and I met at Great Aunt Hildy's funeral a couple of years ago. You gave me your business card and said when I graduated from college I should look you up..."

"Were you wearing a black dress that day?"

"Um, yes, I was wearing a black dress that day...because, y'know, it was a funeral..."

"The short one, right?"

I was confused. Did he mean my black dress was short or I was short?

"I am pretty short," I said.

"Ahh, you're Gilbert's granddaughter!" Uncle Monty said with certainty.

"No, Uncle Monty, I'm Gilbert's great-niece too. I'm Clarabelle's granddaughter. That's me."

"Yes, yes, that's what I meant. Of course I know you. I'm your Uncle Monty! So, what do you need, Jen?"

"Um, well, at the funeral, you said I should look you up after graduation and...it's June, so..."

"So, you've graduated and you need me to help you find a job at my firm?" Uncle Monty said.

"Yes, please," I said, relieved he finally knew who I was.

Uncle Monty didn't waste any time calling in a favor for me, because after all, we were family—even if he couldn't quite place *how* we were related. Within a day I was being interviewed, and by the end of the week I was hired and given the immensely impressive title "Proofreader I" and a ridiculously pitiful salary that made me reconsider just how bad my ass would look in tan polyester. I was a bit disappointed because I had many friends who were making a lot more than me. True, those friends didn't have degrees in creative writing. That might have been a *bit* of my problem with finding a high-paying job. Oh well, I figured, it was still better than smelling like microwave burritos.

My dad reinstated my AmEx once he heard how little I was going to make. ("For gas and work clothes," he said, which I took to mean, "For bars and restaurants.")

I started my first real grown-up job in such a flurry of activity, I don't actually remember much, except that this would go down in history as the worst job I've *ever* had.

Now, let me just stop right there before you start writing me letters. Yes, yes, I've heard of coal miners and ditch diggers and sweatshop workers. I know they have hard jobs and it's very bold of me to say Proofreader I was the worst job I ever had. Well, did I ever say I was a commercial fisherman? Did I ever say I once had a job shearing sheep in the Outback in the dead of summer? No, I didn't. My job history up until that point included babysitting and writing for my college alumni magazine. I am like veal. I have never even waited tables or worked in a fast-food restaurant. My hands are doughy and would be softer if I used moisturizer more often, but I'm too lazy to put lotion on. What I'm trying to say here is, to me, Proofreader I was the worst job I've ever had because I've never been a Rocky Mountain Oyster taste tester.

Let me try to set the scene for you: I worked in the bowels of an enormous building in a drab office park in suburban Kansas. The Proofreading department was housed in the dank, windowless basement. We had our own entrance at the rear of the building so that we wouldn't dare come through the beautiful, well-lit lobby five floors above us. Our department ran twenty-four hours a day, because we were vital to the organization. (Just ask us—we would tell you how vital, mostly because no one else would.) Proposals, letters, contracts, engineering specs—all of it ran through Proofreading, and since it was a global company, there was always work to do no matter what time of day.

The engineers hated our department because we were overhead. We didn't bring in any income to the firm and we billed their projects for our time. There was always a lot of grumbling about how the engineers didn't need us, because computers could do the same job, but better and faster. On my first day of training, my manager Carol warned about the complaining engineers.

"You can't listen to them, Jen. We are essential to this organization. Deals depend upon us. Every time one of the engineers tells me that our department is worthless or archaic and that computers can do it better I show them this," said Carol, handing me a laminated piece of paper. It was a single sheet from a hundred-page proposal for a power plant in India. I could see someone had gone wild with a yellow highlighter all over the page. "About a year ago, a group upstairs put this proposal together and decided they didn't have the money in their budget for Proofreading. They used *spell check* instead. Look what happened."

I looked closer. "Whorehouse" was a word that was highlighted at least half a dozen times on the page.

Carol nodded her head. "You see that? They had a misspelling of 'warehouse' and spell check suggested 'whorehouse' and some idiot said 'OK' and 'change all' and this is what happened. They turned in a hundred-page proposal with the word whorehouse throughout. Can you believe it? Unsurprisingly, they did *not* get the job and our CEO was not very happy with their budget cuts. Now *everyone* understands our value—especially the CEO!"

I understood what Carol was saying, but I wanted to say, *Yeah, if we're so valuable then why are we relegated to the shadows?* Instead, I just nodded and tried to match Carol's pissed-off looks. Carol was my first experience with the "down with the Man" mentality and I didn't have my "fuck the establishment" face mastered yet the way I do now.

The proofreaders worked in pairs in a room full of tiny windowless offices. Each office had metal walls and a desk with two chairs on either side. We didn't get our own cubicle or even our own desk assigned to us, because the powers that be thought it would be better if we changed partners and cubicles every week. They thought we'd make fewer mistakes if we didn't get too comfortable, and it would cut down on the chitchat, because we couldn't get too chummy. So every Friday we would take down our calendars, project billing sheets, family pictures, cat posters, etc., from the metal walls and put them in our little plastic cubby (that we had to bring from home—fucking cheap bastards) filled with our company-issue pens and pencils, so we'd be ready to move on Monday.

Because this was my first job, I didn't yet know anything about office politics. Since that job I have worked with some of the most impressive names in business—Fortune 500 CEOs, government officials, celebrities—but the office politics those guys played were nothing compared to the psychological warfare in Proofreading.

As Proofreader I, I was the lowest of the low. Proofreader IIs had all the power (plus an extra two bucks an hour). Even though we weren't allowed to have permanent cubicles, a couple of them decided that they would. They'd been there longer than Carol, and frankly, she was terrified of them. So when they set up shop and told their partners to come to them, no one even tried to argue. Their cat posters weren't going anywhere and their kids' pictures were in frames hanging on the walls. The message was clear. The IIs were there to stay.

This bold act of defiance gave confidence to some more experienced Proofreader I's who were on the bubble of being promoted. They decreed they now had favorite chairs, and while they would change desks every Monday morning, their chair of choice was coming with them and woe to the proofreader who accidentally touched her precious fucking chair.

I needed a flow chart to remember everyone's preferences and I didn't feel like losing my head over a stupid chair, so I solved this problem by lollygagging with my "Hang in there!" cat posters. I'd fuss over hanging them and then rehanging them until everyone had clocked in and then I'd go find whatever chair was left. My ass just wasn't that picky—unless we're talking about tan polyester.

This company was run like a cross between some fictional dystopian world and a Soviet Bloc prison. There was always someone watching you, grading you, waiting to rat you out for some minor infraction like taking more than the "company-suggested" (i.e., mandatory) two-minute bathroom break. *Of course* we only got two minutes to go the bathroom, because this company was run by men who can whip it out and get the job done in thirty seconds. Hey assholes, it takes me a lot more than two minutes just to pee, wipe properly, and fight to get my "company-suggested" (i.e., mandatory) pantyhose back up!

People in the hallways constantly challenged you about your destination. "Headed somewhere?" a guy with a pocket protector and a short-sleeved dress shirt would ask.

"Need something?" a woman in tan hose and sensible shoes would question.

"Where do you need to be?" a manager-type would inquire.

It was soul-sucking.

One of the most closely guarded places in the building was the Supply Room. And rightly so, in my opinion, because if there is one thing you should know about me it is that my name is Jen and I'm an office-supply stealer and hoarder (*"Hi, Jen"*). Thumbing through corporate supply catalogs gives me a rush. I get high off pictures of purple gel pens. I get chills from high-capacity staplers. There isn't a label maker out there that I don't covet. I huff copy toner.

The Supply Room was also in the basement. The way it was situated reminded me of a pharmacy: a large window and a counter with rows and rows of shelves behind it overflowing with my drug of choice. The only way to get supplies was to bring an official supply request (supply rec) that was filled out in triplicate and signed by your manager and your manager's manager. Three very pretty girls worked the Supply Room and they ruled that place like the Mean Girls' table in the high school lunchroom. Very rarely did a proofreader need anything from the Supply Room. We were not allowed to have staplers or label makers. We didn't have printers so we didn't need paper or toner. We never needed a ruler, a pair of scissors, or even a tape dispenser. All we had were our "Blood Pens," as we called them. Really they were red Pilot Liquid Ink pens. The barrels of the pens were clear so you could see the red ink flow back and forth, thus the "blood." Because our edits and changes had to stand out for the typing pool to see, we were given these fancy red pens. Every other pen in the Supply Room was a piece of crap blue Paper Mate. Only proof-readers—even the lowliest ones like me—got Blood Pens.

We had to guard our pens with our lives, because the engineers were always trying to steal them from us. They'd come down to see us with a quick question about an edit we made or some lame-ass story like that and they'd casually say, "I see. That makes sense. Can I just borrow your pen real quick so I can write that down?" Then they'd take our Blood Pen and divert us with a few more questions and maybe even compliment our hair or something and then POOF! They'd be gone. Five minutes later a new document would come across our desk and we'd reach for our Blood Pen and it was nowhere to be found. *Son of a bitch!*

You probably don't think that's a big deal. *Just go to the Supply Room and get another one, Jen!* Ha. If only it were that easy! Remember what I said about supply recs? You needed your manager and your manager's manager to sign off, and it was nearly impossible to get them to sign anything

together, especially when it was for a Blood Pen. The rumor
was those pens cost the company six bucks each, which was
a fortune to those cheap assholes, and so the only way you
could get another one was to bring your signed supply rec
*and* your empty Blood Pen to the Supply Room. (Yup, they
required you to turn in the empty carcass of your old pen so
that they could "inventory" it. *WTF?*) And if you
complained, it didn't matter. The managers didn't care that
it got stolen. They felt like it was the proofreader's responsibility to guard her company property and if she couldn't do
that, then she was shit out of luck.

The first (and only) time my Blood Pen was stolen was
after a few weeks on the job. Uncle Monty came down and
brought a new engineer with him. They stopped in to chat
me up and the new guy complimented me on my pen.

"Where can I get one of those?" he asked.

"You can't. They're for proofreaders only."

"Bullshit. I'm a project manager. If I want a red pen, I
should be allowed to have one!"

I shrugged my shoulders. I couldn't argue with his logic,
but what did I know? Earlier that week I had discovered
that the newest guy in the mailroom was making more
money than me and he was still trying to finish his GED
with little success! I *had* to get out of this backassward joint!
*Maybe QT is still hiring*, I thought to myself.

"Monty, help me out here," he said. "Where do I get
one of these?"

"You have to go to Supply, but Jen's right. Only Proofreading gets them."

"Well, then give me yours and just go get yourself
another," the guy said to me.

"I can't. I have to turn in my dried-out pen in order to
get another. It's our responsibility if they get stolen. Some

proofreaders don't even leave them in their cubbies overnight. They take them home with them."

"That's ridiculous! It's just a stupid pen."

"It sure is. A few guys up on ten go in together and buy a box from Staples and split the cost," Uncle Monty said. "I've never done it, because the pens are close to ten dollars apiece or something like that."

"Six," I said.

"Either way. Too expensive for me. I'll stick with the company-issue Paper Mate. It's good enough for me!" said Uncle Monty.

"Huh. I was at Supply earlier today. I think that one blonde has a bit of a thing for me. I bet I could get her to give me a red pen," the new guy said.

"Ha! Good luck. Those girls are total bitches. They're used to dealing with super nerds who practically wet themselves from the attention they give them," I said.

Looking back, I think this was probably the moment the new guy decided to steal my pen. It's never wise to call someone, either directly or indirectly, a "super nerd" and then not expect payback.

"Well, what is the pen called?" New Guy asked.

"Pilot Liquid Ink pens," I said.

"Hmm...that's a lot to remember. Can I borrow your pen to write that down?" While he scribbled gibberish on a scrap of paper, he went on. "Has anyone ever told you have really beautiful eyes?"

"Oh...uh...I mean, wow. Thank you," I stammered. Up until that point, the only people who had ever commented about my "beautiful eyes" were my grandparents. I have never been that girl who gets unsolicited compliments from strangers. No one has driven past me and wolf-whistled out the car window. The only time men spoke to me was when they accidentally bumped into me because they failed to look where they were going. I wasn't a troll or anything, but I was no great beauty either. I closely resembled a Cabbage Patch kid and I don't think too many men are on the lookout for apple-cheeked, frizzy-haired, freckle-faced girls to date. Even though I knew all of this, I still let myself fantasize that maybe, just maybe, this cute guy could see through my glasses and slouchy sweaters and sensible shoes and know that inside I was *ah-may-zing*.

"Your eyes really pop against your hair color."

I felt a hot blush creeping up my cheeks. "Thanks," I mumbled.

"You should wear purple more often. It really accentuates your eyes, your hair, your skin tone. It's perfect."

"Uhhh..." I didn't know what to say at that point. How did girls deal with this kind of stuff on a daily basis? I was so flustered I couldn't form a complete sentence. I just mumbled and stuttered my way through a word salad combination. You would think I might have realized something was afoot at that point, but no, I didn't.

"Oh crap! Look at the time, Monty! We need to get back up for that meeting with Monroe or we're gonna be late. Thanks for your help, Jen. I really appreciate it. And hey," he said, looking deeply into my (beautiful) eyes while surreptitiously pocketing my pen, "I'll see you real soon." And then he and my Blood Pen were gone.

That night I stopped by the office supply store on my way home and shelled out twenty-five hard-earned dollars for a box of Blood Pens. The joke was on the firm, though, because I ran a black market supply store out of my cubby and charged those thieving engineers five bucks a pen. They never knew I only paid two.

THE NEW YORK YEARS

# CHAPTER 4

## THANKS FOR INTERVIEWING
## ME AND MY HIDEOUS NOSE

IT WAS 1997ish and I was in between jobs. I'd been "downsized" (i.e., fired) from the engineering firm (not sure what I did wrong exactly, but I think it was related to my illegal black market office supply store) and I was searching for my next McJob when I decided to take a huge leap.

The year before, I'd logged onto AOL and met the most interesting cheap bastard on the internet and I was falling hard. Ebeneezer lived in New York City and I was in Kansas City. It was hard to make the relationship work when we were so far apart. We'd been doing the long-distance dating thing, but we finally decided it was time to make our relationship legit: one of us needed to move. I was living in suburban Kansas City with only my mother and father to hang out with. Ebeneezer was living in his parents' basement in New York City. Neither person's situation seemed terrific to the other. However, since I was the one out of work, I announced that I'd be the one to move (just not to his parents' basement). I was nervous though. Up until that point, we'd never spent more than about four days in a row in the same place and I was worried that once we were together all the time, maybe we'd see that we were both horrible people and we would break up. I didn't want to get dumped and then run the risk of bumping into my ex in the relatively small metropolis of Kansas City. But, I reasoned, if we broke up in New York City, I could disappear into a crowd of seven million people and live out my dream as one of those writer-types you always see on TV living in fabulous shabby-chic, rent-controlled apartments with enormous walk-in closets. That seemed *totally* possible. So, I jumped at the chance to move.

I wanted to have a job before I relocated, but it seemed impossible. I spent a small fortune buying the Sunday *New York Times*, so I could literally circle want ads with my Blood Pen. I was burning up my dad's fax machine sending out resumes, but hardly anyone was responding. I applied for a bunch of jobs, but no one really wanted to talk to me on the phone. They all wanted to interview me in person. I finally got one human resources manager who agreed to talk to me over the phone.

"It's that you're not here. We're not sure you're serious about making the move," she told me.

"I'm serious, but I can't make the move until I have a job," I argued.

"I understand, but it just doesn't work that way. You need to take the leap and come here and then you'll get interviews."

"You're sure?" I asked.

"I'm positive," she said. "Your resume is good. It's just the fact that you're in Kansas that's making it difficult. I'd interview you if you came."

"Okay, thanks," I said.

There was nothing I could do except take the chance and move across the country and hope someone hired me. I explained my predicament to my parents, and I didn't know if they were just eager to be rid of me or if they really believed in me. Either way, they helped me make the move.

I was in my early twenties, so I didn't need my parents' "permission," but it helped greatly to have their blessing—and support. My mom flew out to New York and spent a weekend with me searching to find the best (and safest) apartment we could locate. And then she also cosigned the lease for me since I was unemployed. I packed up my futon, my boom box, and my leather briefcase and moved to Queens. Sure, I didn't have any job prospects, but I was young and dumb (and sort of in love) and I figured jobs would magically appear—somehow. My parents, God bless them, didn't say a word to me. I can't even believe it now when I look back. On the outside they were like, "Yeah, you'll be great, kid. Don't worry." Inside they were probably dying. They had to have been. Either that or my dad was totally turning my bedroom into a library in his mind.

I immediately started answering want ads but it quickly became apparent that my English degree was, once again, not in great demand. I was surprised, because New York was the land of publishing. I was positive that Random House or Simon & Schuster needed me. How could they not? I was a shoo-in. Think about it: I loved to read and talk about books. I thought, *What else is there to do at a publishing house?* Unfortunately, most of the publishing houses were like, "Yeah, we prefer Ivy Leaguers. And we do a lot more than just read books, Jen."

I started getting nervous; my rent was due and I needed to find something fast or else I'd be back in Kansas before you could say "flying monkeys." I took a close look at my list of applications and decided I'd been too picky. I was consumed with looking for a job that I "loved" and a job that could be a "career," and that wasn't going to cut it anymore. Desperate times called for desperate measures. So instead of reading job descriptions, I started skimming the ads for salary. I needed a certain amount to pay my bills and I was willing do anything—well, almost anything—if the money was right. I could find a career later.

I was skimming pretty hard one day when one of the job descriptions caught my eye. It didn't sound sexy, but I had all the skills necessary (organized, self-motivated, attention to detail, the usual bullshit), the money was good (really good), and it was close to my apartment. So I faxed over a resume and by lunchtime I had a call back.

"Hello, this is Doctor Finkelman's office," the woman said. "You sent us a resume."

"Yes, hello," I said, scouring the spreadsheet I'd made listing all of the resumes I'd sent out (because I'm damn organized). I found it: Dr. Finkelman, plastic surgeon, seeking office manager, good money, excellent benefits, close to home.

"Dr. Finkelman would like to set up a time to interview you."

"Great!" I said, grabbing my calendar. "When? I have some time this afternoon."

"No," she said. "It can't be during regular business hours. He's very busy. He prefers to meet candidates after patient hours. He can meet you tomorrow night at his office."

"Okay," I said. "What time?"

"Eleven," she said.

"Excuse me?" I asked, putting down my pencil. "I thought you said he needed to meet after work."

"Yes, he can meet with you at eleven p.m. at his office."

"Eleven p.m.?" I asked. What the fuck? Who meets prospective office workers at eleven at night?

"Yes. Is that a problem for you?" the woman asked. "Because we do have other applicants."

I looked at my calendar. I had five more days until my rent was due, my bank account was dwindling, I had credit card bills to pay. I needed a job soon. I would have to meet him at eleven. "No, it's fine. I can do that. Will you be there too?" I asked, hoping she'd say yes. I wasn't exactly scared, but I was weirded out and I would have felt better if she said she was going to be there too.

The woman scoffed. "Of course not. Dr. Finkelman does not need my opinion."

"Right," I said. "Okay, thanks."

That night when Ebeneezer came over for dinner I told him about my good news. "I have an interview tomorrow."

"Oh yeah?" he said, shoveling chicken into his mouth. "Mrgrhg?"

"What?"

He swallowed. "What's the job?"

"Office manager."

Ebeneezer frowned. "I thought you wanted to write."

"I know, but I'm not getting any calls for writing jobs."

"Okay, office manager isn't so bad. I guess. When's the interview?"

"Eleven...at night."

He stopped eating. "Eleven o'clock at night?" he asked.

"Yeah." I shrugged. "That's not *so* weird, right?"

"Jen, it's *really* weird. Who meets people at eleven at night?"

"I don't know. This guy does."

"What does he even do?" Ebeneezer asked.

"He's a very busy doctor. His assistant said that he could only meet after business hours."

"Okay, so even seven o'clock would be after his office closes. Why does it need to be so late?"

"I have no idea, Ebeneezer," I said, exasperated. "I just know I need a job, and no one else is calling me, not even that HR manager who promised she'd interview me if I moved here—bitch—and so I'm going."

"Well, you're not going alone," he said. "I'll take you."

"Oh my God, you cannot take me!" I said. "How creepy is that? Hi, I'm here for the job and this is my psycho controlling boyfriend who goes everywhere with me."

"It's not like that! I'll take you and I'll wait outside for you. He will never even know I'm there. Believe me, you want me there. This guy could be a serial killer or something."

The next night, Ebeneezer borrowed his parents' car and drove me to my interview. We arrived at Dr. Finkelman's office a half hour early. Ebeneezer wanted to case out the joint. Make sure it seemed on the up and up. It was a small medical building on a quiet street. The sign out front indicated that Dr. Finkelman occupied the whole building.

"Nice place," Ebeneezer said. "What kind of doctor is he again?"

"Plastic surgeon."

"Hmm, no wonder he can pay you so much."

"Yeah, the pay is really good."

"But maybe the hours suck. What if you have to work until eleven at night, Jen? When will we see each other?"

I shrugged. "I don't know. His assistant doesn't work that late. I guess that's something I'll have to talk to Finkelman about. Let me get an offer first and then I'll worry about my hours," I said.

"Yeah, because I don't like the idea of you working this late and then catching a bus home. It's unsafe. The guy is probably bizarre. You know that, right?"

"Well, if he's creepy, I'll just leave. I want to hear what he has to say. I need—"

"The money." Ebeneezer sighed. "I know, Jen. I know."

"Well, I can't stay in New York if I can't pay my bills."

"I hear you, but you've got plenty of reserves. You don't have to take the first job that's offered to you. You'll get other offers," Ebeneezer assured me. "Especially if this guy is a lunatic or something."

I glanced at the clock. "It's time. I need to go." I gathered my fancy leather briefcase and my purse and stepped out of the car.

"If it seems strange in there, don't be afraid to kick him in the balls and run," Ebeneezer said. "I'll be right outside."

I laughed. "I doubt it's going to come to that. Don't worry...but thanks for the advice."

I walked up to the front door of the building. The vestibule was dark. I pulled on the door, half expecting it to be locked, because who the fuck works at eleven o'clock at night? The door opened silently and I stepped into the darkness. There was a door at the far end of the hall with a sliver of light shining underneath. Was that where I was supposed to go? There were no indications of where I should be. I figured the least Dr. Finkelman could do would be to meet me in the hall and show me in. *Ugh.*

I knocked on the door and then opened it. I was in a small, scruffy waiting room with dog-eared magazines and worn, mismatched plastic chairs. The guy was offering me a great deal of money to run his office, but his waiting room made it look like he couldn't afford the light bill. I was immediately suspicious. "Hello?" I called. "Dr. Finkelman?

Are you here?" I listened, but the place was silent. I didn't know what to do. Yes, I needed a job, but come on, did I need a job this bad? Ebeneezer was right. I did have plenty in the bank, I just didn't want to use it. Did I really need to roam around an empty doctor's office late at night hoping to bump into the very busy Dr. Finkelman? Earlier that day I'd received a call back on another resume I'd sent out. It wasn't as lucrative as Dr. Finkelman's position, but maybe I should take that job instead. "Oh this is ridiculous," I muttered. I was tired, it was way past my bedtime and I wanted to get the hell out of there. I turned to go and I found Dr. Finkelman standing silently behind me. "Oh my God!" I yelped.

"I'm sorry," he said, holding up his hands. "I didn't mean to scare you. I was in the bathroom and didn't hear you come in. I'm Dr. Finkelman." He stuck out his hand.

"Jen Mann," I said, shaking his hand and hoping to God he was a post-pee hand-washer.

"Let's go in my office, please, Jen. We can chat there."

I followed him to the back of the building, past several closed doors. He opened a door to reveal a small closet-like office. "Here we go," he said. "Sit, sit." He motioned to a plastic chair.

I sat.

He slumped behind the desk and rubbed his eyes. He looked very tired. His desk was covered with stacks of folders and loose papers. "Now," he said, "let me see if I can find your resume." He made an attempt to search through the papers strewn everywhere.

"I have an extra copy if that would help," I said, reaching into my briefcase.

He smiled. "Ah," he said. "Nicely done. You *are* prepared and organized!"

I smiled. Let me just say that my house is always a shit-pile. My bed is never made, my clothes are rarely hung up and the dishes are always dirty. But when it comes to my business side, I am organized as fuck. I take that shit seriously. "Of course," I said, handing him the paper.

Dr. Finkelman barely glanced at the resume that had taken me hours to perfect. Just the week before I'd asked Ebeneezer, "Do you think I should say I can *implement* new office procedures or I can *execute* new office procedures?"

"Is there a difference?" Ebeneezer had asked.

"Looks fine, looks fine," Dr. Finkelman said, discarding the paper. "Okay, let me tell you about the job. Basically, I have an incredibly busy practice and I need someone to manage my office and my staff. I'm the boss, but really, you'd be the boss. You would manage the staff, you would do the hiring and firing, you would make sure patients pay us, that our bills get paid, all of it. You need to make sure that all I have to do is be a doctor. Does that sound good?"

I nodded. Psht, any job where I get to boss people around has always sounded good to me.

"Now, you know the salary. I put it in the ad, because I just wanted to get it out in the open. You're fine with the pay?"

"Well, it depends on the hours..." I said.

"You'd be here seven in the morning to seven at night Monday to Friday. You get all the government holidays off with pay plus a couple more weeks as well. I'm Orthodox and my office is closed for all Jewish holidays."

"Do I get Christmas off?" I asked. "I have to be home for Christmas. My mom will kill me if I'm not. She's kind of a freak about Christmas."

"Yes, yes," he said. "You'll be home. No problem. You

get paid vacation too, of course. And then there are the perks."

"The perks?" I asked, confused.

"The perks of working for a plastic surgeon," Dr. Finkelman said, smiling. "Anything you want done. I'll fix it. No charge. It's part of your package. In fact, I insist. I like my staff to be walking billboards."

"Anything I want fixed?" I asked. I was of course thinking about my breasts. My melons, my knockers, my bazooms. Ever since they debuted when I was twelve I had been looking for a way to get rid of them. "Like my boobs? You could make them smaller?"

"Your breasts?" Dr. Finkelman said. He ogled my chest, but in a professional way. He shrugged. "Yeah, okay. Are they giving you trouble?"

"Well, like back pain?" I asked.

"Yes."

"No, but they're bigger than I'd like," I said.

"Hmm." He frowned. "Are you married?"

I was shocked. What kind of question was that? What did that have to do with my breasts? "No," I said.

"Yeah, then maybe wait to get that done. Your husband, he might not want them to change. Never saw a husband who asked for his wife to get smaller breasts. Never. No, I would start with your nose."

"My nose?" I blinked rapidly and tried not to look offended. Sure, my nose had always been a bit of a beak, but I don't know that I'd list it as my number one problem. "My nose is bad?"

"It's okay. I can fix it, no problem. It's a very easy procedure. I can do it in my sleep. And the results are fantastic. You won't recognize yourself. It will be so much better."

"My nose needs to be fixed so much that I would be

unrecognizable after surgery?" I asked. I rubbed my misshapen nose, reassuring the lump across my bridge that she wasn't going anywhere.

"And then, of course, there's your chin."

"My chin?!" I exclaimed. Sure. Okay. The boobs I had always thought were too much. Even the nose I could see, but I had never even considered my chin before. "There's something wrong with my chin?"

"Well, once we fix the nose, then everyone will notice your chin. We'll need to get it into proportion. And it could be daintier. You have a large chin."

I was more than a little horrified at what he was suggesting. "I don't mind my nose...or my chin," I said meekly.

"Really? Huh." He seemed genuinely shocked. "What about your eyes?"

"My eyes are my best feature!" I said. Now I was practically crying. "My boyfriend told me he fell in love with me because of my eyes and my brain."

Dr. Finkelman looked at me skeptically and I saw his eyes slip down to my chest—in a non-professional way. "If that's what he said, then who am I to argue?"

By then I was in the throes of self-hatred, so I had to know, "Okay, what's wrong with my eyes?"

"Nothing, really. They could just use a little tweak is all. Nothing drastic. A little lift, maybe a little tightening in the corners. What are you, now, thirty?"

"I'm only twenty-five!"

"Hmm, well you have some excess skin that tends to get worse with age. We could hold off a year or two, but I wouldn't recommend pushing it past that."

"Wow," I said, slumping in my seat.

"Plus, your brows could use some work."

I rubbed my eyebrows self-consciously. "They just need

a wax," I whimpered. I could see Dr. Finkelman eyeing my ears and I pulled my hair over them before he could tell me they were deformed.

He clapped his hands together sharply and exhaled. "So? What do you think? Do you want the job?"

Just moments before, the job he had described sounded great. I would make good money, I would get tons of days off, I would get to boss people around, and I could have all the free surgery my grotesque body needed. Too bad all it cost me was every last ounce of my already depleted self-esteem.

I was instantly aware of my overtaxed bra strap digging painfully into my shoulder. *How ironic,* I thought. *The one part of my body that I want to change he won't do because my future husband might be a boob man.* I narrowed my droopy eyes and took a deep breath through my misshapen nose and exhaled it through my razor-thin lips (he hadn't mentioned my hideous lips specifically, but I figured if I was going under the knife, I might as well get my lips plumped too) before I spoke. "Um, well, I'm going to need to think about it," I said.

He nodded. "Well, don't think too long. I'm filling this position by Friday."

"I'll be in touch," I said, gathering my things.

Dr. Finkelman escorted me to the door. "Thanks for coming in, Jen. It was a real pleasure," he said, extending his hand.

I shook his hand. "Thank you."

I turned to leave and he fired his final arrow into me. "Oh! I forgot! This might help you decide!" he said. "We can, of course, do lipo. You're clearly a terrific candidate for it."

"Of course I am," I mumbled, instinctively sucking in my gelatinous gut.

By the time I flung myself into the car, I was practically in tears.

"What happened in there?" Ebeneezer exclaimed. "Are you okay? Did he hurt you?"

"Not physically," I said. I faced him and asked, "Ebeneezer, you love me for my eyes and my brain, right?"

His eyes slipped down to my breasts, ogling me in a non-professional way. "Um, yeah, sure, of course," he mumbled.

I didn't accept the job with Dr. Finkelman. My self-esteem couldn't have survived. I also never got my breasts reduced, because my relationship wouldn't have survived either. Apparently Ebeneezer could overlook my repulsive nose, chin, and eyes, but smaller boobs were a deal breaker.

## CHAPTER 5

### IF YOU WORK IN THE DUNGEON, CAN YOU STILL CALL IT A DREAM JOB?

AFTER THE MEETING with Dr. Finkelman did not go as I had hoped and I had turned down his generous offer to reduce my boobs (with my husband's permission, of course), fix my horrible nose, and suck the fat out of my back, I used my flabby fingers to send out even more resumes. By that point, I figured my resume was sitting on the fax machine of every human resources department on Manhattan Island. Luckily I got a call a few days later from a woman named Carla.

Carla had run an ad in the paper that I answered. I don't remember what it said—probably something like, "Are you hardworking, independent, and bright? Do you go above and beyond and sweat the details? Interesting, high-paying, and exciting work available. College degree preferred" or some kind of nondescript, horoscope-like ad. It was like a horoscope because it could fit anyone. She never told you anything about the job; she totally played to your ego. Who sits there and thinks, "Nah, I'm not too bright. I'd better not apply for this one" or "I dunno, do I really want a high-paying and exciting job?" Even the college degree thing. It was just "preferred" but not mandatory. After reading the ad five times, I still had no idea what the job entailed, but I knew I wanted it! So I faxed off my resume to Carla without a clue as to what she was offering. I probably figured anything was better than getting free cheek implants.

"This Jen from Kansas?" she asked in a thick New Yawk accent.

"Yes, speaking," I said.

"This is Carla from Pro Placements. I got your resume and I like it a lot. Can you come in and talk to me?"

"Um, what is the job, exactly?" I asked, scrolling frantically through my spreadsheet and trying to remember even the slightest detail, but there was nothing to remember because the ad had been so damn vague. I finally found her listing: *Carla, Pro Placements, high-paying and exciting, must type.*

"I have a lot of them," Carla replied. "See, I'm a recruiter. I fill all kinds of positions."

My rube antenna went up. I was from Kansas, but I wasn't going to get snookered on my first day. I wasn't going to be the sap who bought the Brooklyn Bridge. "What will this cost me?" I asked warily.

Carla chuckled. "Nah, it doesn't work like that," she assured me. "The company pays me once I match them to the right employee."

"So it's free for me?"

"Yeah, completely."

"No risk?" I asked.

"The only risk is finding a terrific career," Carla said, sounding only a little bit like a used-car salesman.

"Are they good companies?" I asked, still wary.

"Some of the best," Carla said. "Look, you're not working now, right?"

"No," I admitted.

"Okay, I can also hook you up with a temp job."

"What's a temp job?"

"Really?"

"I've heard of them, but I really don't know what that means."

"So lots of companies have openings they can't fill with permanent people for one reason or another. Maybe someone's out on maternity leave or on vacation or maybe they just don't want to pay for benefits. They tell me what openings they have and I send them bodies. You make decent money without the stress of being a regular employee. You clock in, do your work, and clock out. No hassle. It's short-term, so you don't have office politics to deal with and that sort of thing. You can still interview for full-time work but make some money while you're waiting for the perfect job opening."

"Wow, that does sound great," I said, relaxing.

"Yeah," Carla said. "Can you type?"

"I can."

"Are you fast?"

I was not a mathlete in school, nor was I valedictorian. But there was one class I excelled at. No, not gym class. I was a ridiculous typist. I won every stupid award my typing teacher would come up with. "Ninety words a minute," I bragged. I refrained from telling Carla I had received the Flying Fingers Awards in both '89 *and* '90.

"I'll test you," Carla warned me. "Don't lie."

"I'm not lying. I'll ace it," I assured her.

"Come see me as soon as you can."

Later that afternoon I found myself in a dumpy office building in Midtown Manhattan. I stepped off the elevator on the third floor and found myself engulfed in a cacophony. The room was filled with desks lined up in neat rows and at each desk was a twenty- or thirty-something noisily working the phones.

A young man with his feet on the desk was crowing into his phone, "I'm telling you, Jimmy, you're gonna love my guy. He's got the goods. You saw his resume. He's the one."

"Mary, Mary, I hear you," said a young woman with the phone wedged between her ear and her shoulder. She was hunched over a takeout container of sushi and she was taking bites in between words. "Okay, fine, she wasn't the best, but listen, I just got a new client today. She is stellar. I'm telling you. You're going to die when you meet her. Let me just see if I can get her over there before end of business today and we can wrap this up."

The receptionist looked up from a *People* magazine that was splayed out in front of her. She didn't speak. She just raised one bored eyebrow.

"I'm here to see Carla."

"She says you gotta take the test first," the receptionist said.

"The typing test?"

"All of them," she sighed, flipping the magazine shut. "Follow me."

She took me to a small conference room. Inside were six computers arranged in a square around the room. Four of them had applicants hunched over them, nervously pecking at the keyboards.

"No talking," she said. "Instructions are there on the

wall. The test is timed and you can't back up. Once you mark your answer, it will be final. Carla will get your scores and then she'll talk to you...maybe." She turned on her heel and left, closing the door behind her.

I glanced around the room, but no one looked up from their computer. I sat down silently and studied the laminated instructions taped to the wall behind the computer. They didn't really tell me much more than the receptionist had. I took a deep breath and I hit the start button.

The first test was PowerPoint. "Fuck," I muttered. I mean, yes, I'd put PowerPoint on my resume. I said I could work all of the Microsoft Office products, but I'd never actually used PowerPoint. I figured if it came down to it in a work situation, I'd be able to fake it until I could grab the manual for a quick peek or I could farm out the work to someone else. Unfortunately there was no manual or sucker to pawn off the work to, so I had to dive in. It was a little messy, but I got through it. I couldn't make the damn tiles fly in from the left, only the right. The next one was Excel. I loved spreadsheets. I used them for everything, so I made that test my bitch. Then it was time for Word. *No problem,* I thought as I cut and pasted with keyboard shortcuts and saved and ran spell-checks and generated mailing lists. *I've got this.*

Finally, it was time for the typing test—the Big Dance. *Oh yeah,* I thought. *Bring it on.*

Now that I'm in my forties, I know that hubris is a very dangerous thing. Now that I'm in my forties, I never feel cocksure about anything, but especially not about anything I'm being tested on. And even if I'm a teensy bit confident about my abilities, I still keep that shit under wraps, because the universe loves to fuck you up. But as a twenty-something, I wasn't as wise as I am now, and so I think I literally cracked my knuckles like a TV villain and looked around the room silently mocking everyone else in there. *See ya, suckers,* I probably thought. *Watch me burn up this keyboard with my ah-may-zing keystroke skills. Don't blink or else you're going to miss the show.*

The screen lit up with giant numbers counting down the time to the beginning of the test. *Five, four...* I looked around frantically. I was starting to panic. I couldn't find what I was supposed to type. *Three, two...* Where the fuck was the paper I was to copy from? "Wait!" I said. "Wait!"

"Shhhh!" the girl next to me said.

"Where's the paper for the typing test? What do I type?"

"No talking!" the girl hissed.

*ONE! GO!* My computer screen screamed at me. Precious seconds ticked by and I still could not see what I was supposed to type.

Then, finally, I spotted it—a paragraph on the bottom of the instructions taped to the wall. The instructions I obviously had not read carefully (so much for that "attention to detail" bullet point I put on my resume). *Shit.* The wall seemed far away and the print was so small. I was struggling. The typing test ran a clock stopwatch-style in the bottom corner and I found myself watching it, mesmerized by it, rather than typing. *Get to work!* my brain screamed. I told my fingers to fly, but they sort of flopped around the keyboard. I quickly realized that it had been a long time since the fall of '90 when I was the reigning typing champ. My skills had atrophied quite a bit during my college years, and since college I'd barely used them. The section on numbers and random punctuation killed me. (How many times do you use a bracket in real life!?) I don't even want to say how long I hunted and pecked for the fucking 9 key. I was dying. Worse, I was failing!

The screen suddenly went dark and a message popped up:

## THANK YOU. PLEASE GO TO RECEPTION AND WAIT TO HEAR YOUR NAME.

*Shit, shit, shit.* I wanted another chance.

"I can do better," I told the bored receptionist.

"You have to wait for Carla," she said.

"I got confused on the typing section. I need to go again."

She looked down at the *People* magazine in front of her. Our conversation was over.

I waited for twenty agonizing minutes until finally a woman about my age with dark black hair tottered into reception on bright red sky-high heels and called my name.

"Hi, I'm Carla," she said, sticking out her hand.

"Hi. Listen, I need to go again."

"Yeah, you bombed it pretty good, Jen. I thought you'd do better."

"I know. So did I. I don't test well. It's, like, a semi-proven thing with me. I know what to expect now. I can wear my glasses this time so I can see the wall better—it was really far away. I don't wear my glasses normally, because you know, glasses, eww, right? But I really needed them. Just let me try again, please."

Carla looked skeptical. "Here's the thing. With the scores you got, I can get you *a job*. But if you can really deliver a higher typing score, I can get you a *good* job. Like a *career* job. Y'know what I'm saying? There's a difference, Jen."

"I do, I so do," I said. "Please."

"All right. One more time. But if you give me sixty-five words a minute again, you're out."

I went back into the testing room. This time my ego was knocked down a few pegs and I was fully prepared with glasses in hand and my head firmly in the game. I ignored the mesmerizing clock and concentrated completely on the task at hand. I even found the 9 with no problem. I also managed to ignore the fact that sixty-five words a minute was not a failing score and anyone who wasn't Carla or my high school typing teacher would be fine with that score!

"One hundred fucking words per minute," Carla said, slapping her hand on her desk. "Unbelievable!"

I smiled. "You should see what I could do if I took that test a third time," I said.

"Don't push your luck, Jen," Carla said. "No one likes a dick."

I should have been offended, but instead I smiled. Carla was totally my people. "I hear you," I said.

She picked up my resume and made some notes in the margins. "Okay, Jenni Mann, tell me what you want to do."

"It's Jen, actually," I mumbled.

"What's that?"

"Well, I took this resume-writing class and they said you should put your legal name on your resume and so I did. My legal name is Jenni with an adorable 'i', but I hate it. I really want to be called Jen."

Carla frowned. "You took a resume-writing class?"

"Yes."

Carla leaned back in her chair and kicked off her heels under her desk. "What else did they teach you?"

"That you should print it on a colored piece of paper to

stand out from a sea of white paper or you should write it with crayon or—"

"Stop. Did you just say write your resume in crayon?" Carla asked.

I was sheepish. "Yes. The instructor said it can show a potential employer that you're fun and creative."

Carla cackled. "Look, Jen, no one wants to hire someone who is fun and creative and writes her resume with a fucking crayon. That doesn't show your fun and creative side. It shows that you're an imbecile who can't afford a pen. Knock that shit off. And colored paper? Really? You faxed me your resume. Pink paper wasn't going to make a difference."

"True," I admitted.

"What else did they suggest? Spritzing perfume on the paper or including a snapshot?"

"Um, actually a photo was suggested. Let them see that you've got a friendly face."

"No one is hiring you for your friendly fucking face, Jen. Tell me you didn't do the photo thing."

"I didn't. I mean, I took one, but it looked like a mug shot," I said. "I thought it would hurt more than help."

"I hope you didn't pay a lot for this resume-writing class," Carla said.

"It was free. My college offered it to the seniors before we graduated."

"Oh, thank God. I was beginning to think you were an idiot."

"No, I'm not an idiot, Carla. I promise," I said.

"Idiots never think they're idiots," Carla said.

I didn't know what to say that wouldn't seem idiotic so I just said, "Fuck off, already."

Carla smiled a giant toothy grin. "All right, let's get to work. I know you're from Kansas. Why did you move here?"

"Real story or fake story?" I asked.

She narrowed her eyes. "Real story first."

"Okay, so I met this guy—Ebeneezer—on the internet about a year ago. He lives here and I was in Kansas. We've been dating long distance, but we wanted to be in the same city. See if this thing is, like, for real. I always wanted to be a writer. Writers live in New York City. So I was the one who moved."

"Ha! I love it. How's it going with him?"

I thought about her question. "Um, it's good. I think. I don't have a lot of experience with boyfriends and so it can feel sort of suffocating sometimes, but I still like to be around him. That's good, right?"

"Don't ask me. I'm happily single," said Carla. "Okay, fake story now."

"I am looking to make my mark on the greatest city in the world. I want to be a valuable asset working for an amazing international company that can only be found in New York City." I shrugged. "Or some shit like that."

Carla laughed. "We can work on that one." She rifled through the enormous piles of paper on her desk. "You're a writer, huh?"

I shrugged. "Kinda."

"You want to work for a magazine? A glossy one?" Carla asked, waving a piece of paper at me.

I sat up straighter in my chair. "Yeah!" I immediately imagined myself writing incredible in-depth feature stories for *Vanity Fair* or travel tips for *Condé Nast Traveler*.

"I've got something here that would work for you. It's a temp job, but they're looking to make it permanent. Basically, if they like you, they'll make you an offer in a month or so."

She showed me the name of the magazine and I immediately swooned in my chair. "I have subscribed to that magazine since I was twelve years old," I said.

"I know, right? Me too. It's a good one. Right now you'll be a temp, but once you get hired, you'll have great benefits and nice perks too. Your scores are perfect. You're just what they want. You can start tomorrow morning. Nine a.m. Look nice, but not too business-y. This is fashion, after all, so be fashionable."

"Right," I said, my stomach sinking. *Fashionable?* Fuck me. I wore overalls on my first date with Ebeneezer. Fashionable was not in my vocabulary. "I'll see what I can come up with."

---

The next day I showed up at the office carrying my most fashion-forward Coach outlet purse and wearing all black. The night before, Ebeneezer and I had decided all black was the most fashionable thing I could swing. My closet was full of prairie skirts and pastel sweater vests, so my one black dress was the least offensive thing I owned. (Looking back, I blame this job for starting my love affair with all black. It's so damn easy and it covers the stains when I drip lunch down my front.)

I greeted the security guard. "Hello, I'm Jen Mann. I'm new. I'm here to see—"

He interrupted me. "Take the west bank of elevators to the basement."

"The basement?" I croaked.

"You said you're Jen Mann, right?"

"Yes."

He consulted the paper in front of him. "Yup, you go to archives. Basement. West elevators." He turned away.

Basement? Again to the basement? *Why are all my jobs located in the basement?* I wondered. My first new *ah-may-zing* and incredible New York City job in fashion and I was being relegated to the basement? "Thank you," I mumbled. He waved me off.

I found the west elevators (after trying to take the east elevators and realizing they didn't go to the bowels of the building; the east only go up) and made my way down, down, down to the archives department. I realized that when I'd accepted the job from Carla, I'd never asked her what the job actually was. Damn her and her wily ways! I knew my hourly wage and I was happy with that, and I knew the name of the magazine and I was thrilled with that, but I never asked what I'd be doing specifically. *Whoops.*

The elevator dumped me into a brightly lit area with high ceilings and lots of empty cubicles. The lobby of the building had been alive with vibrant people, enormous artwork, and lots of sound. This cavernous room was cold and bare and austere and silent. You'd never know you were at a glossy magazine.

A small, round woman greeted me. "Jen?"

I nodded.

"Hello. I'm Margaret. I'm your supervisor. Let's get you started."

Margaret set me up in one of the empty cubicles and explained that my job was to go through endless boxes of contracts and double-check them for accuracy.

"Here is your checklist," she said. "Once you've finished this box, see me, and I'll get you another one. Your lunch is at noon. Call me with any questions."

I sat down and stared at Margaret's list. Some of the questions were so basic, a monkey could do my job. "Oh well, at least it's just temporary," I said.

I began, but after an hour I picked up the phone and called Carla. "This is not going to work for me," I whispered.

"What's the matter?" she snapped.

"I'm in a basement going through fifty-year-old contracts. Half these people are dead. Who cares if they signed their contract in the correct place or not? This is not glamorous. I didn't need to wear all black for this."

Carla sighed. "It's a very impressive place to work, Jen."

"You heard me say I'm in the basement, right?"

"I'll see what I can do. Can you get away for interviews?"

"Of course. I'm a temp." "Okay, well, work hard and do a good job. You're a reflection on me and I don't want to ruin my relationship with Margaret. I'll find you some interviews."

By the end of the day I'd gone through ten boxes. Margaret was impressed. "Wow, you did great," she said.

Yeah, well, it's easy to get a lot of work done when literally no one will talk to you. Seriously. No one would speak to me. The cubicles around me were empty when I started the day, but by ten a.m. they were full of young, impossibly skinny, giggly girls checking contracts. They took coffee breaks and smoke breaks and break breaks every thirty minutes. They flitted around and gossiped with one another, their heels click-clicking on the concrete floor. At one point a rumor that free lipstick was being given out on the tenth floor sent them all scurrying for the elevator. I think one girl's high heels caused her to topple over and the others trampled her, but I can't be sure. At lunchtime, I heard them all making plans to stand outside and eat ice chips and smoke while they smelled the fumes from the pizzeria next door. I decided to take a book and go have some pizza.

"Jen, if you keep this up, I think we could make something permanent for you around here," Margaret said.

My heartbeat quickened. Even though I hated working in the basement and I hated reading contracts, it was a really impressive place to be and maybe I could work my way up the ladder and be a writer someday. I had to start somewhere and maybe the archives was the place to start. "Here in the archives?" I asked, hoping she'd say no.

Margaret nodded. "Yes."

"Does anyone ever...get out...of the archives?" I asked, hesitant because I didn't want to offend Margaret. It was clear that she'd probably been there since the building was built.

Margaret looked sad. "Sometimes," she said. "I think once, maybe."

"Because the thing is, I want to be a writer. I would love to write for this magazine and I'm happy to put in my time, but this job is just...it's..." I struggled for the words, but all I could think was *this job sucks donkey balls.*

"It's steady work," Margaret countered. "A salary and benefits and perks too. Today the girls all got lipstick. That's worth something, right? Once we got shoes, but there weren't any in my size."

Steady work did sound appealing. The threat of eviction was always hanging over my head. Maybe I was being an asshole. A spoiled brat. Margaret was right; it was a fine job and I could probably work my way up. "What's the salary?" I asked.

Margaret pushed a scrap of paper toward me with a

number written on it. A number that confused the hell out of me. "Is that per week?" I asked.

Margaret laughed. "No, that's monthly, Jen."

I looked at the number again. "Monthly?" I screeched. "That's all you pay? You're an international fashion magazine with millions of subscribers and that's what you're offering me?"

"Don't forget the benefits," Margaret reminded me.

"And the free lipstick!" I added.

"Exactly."

"I can't pay my rent in lipstick, Margaret," I said. "How in the hell does anyone afford their rent if this is their salary?"

"Well, uh, I don't know," Margaret said, baffled, because at the end of the day, Margaret was a decently-paid supervisor who didn't give a second thought to the lives of the cogs in the wheel below her.

"I can't take the job," I said. "I can't afford to. I would make double this if I just stayed on and temped for you. You realize that, right? You're paying me more to temp than you're paying your full-time employees."

Margaret looked uncomfortable.

"Look, I'm sorry. Thank you for the offer, but my answer is no. I'll stay on and temp if you want me to, but I'll be interviewing for other positions."

"I see," Margaret said. "That's fine."

A few minutes later I was shutting everything down and getting ready to go home when a gaggle of girls showed up in the opening of my cubicle. "Hi," the tall blonde one said.

"Hi."

"Margaret sent us to talk to you," the short dark-haired one said.

"About what?" I asked.

"About why you should work here."

"Why?"

The blonde shrugged. "I don't know. She likes you or something. Anyway, we're supposed to tell you that you get so much more than just a salary working here."

"Like what? Lipstick?"

The dark-haired one nodded vigorously. "Those lipsticks are like a hundred dollars apiece. We got them for free. I mean, the color is kind of weird, but still, for free."

The redhead piped up. "We also get mascara and eye shadow sometimes. I totally haven't bought any makeup since I started working here."

"Once we got shoes," said the blonde.

"None of them fit Margaret," I said.

"That's because she has a wide foot."

"I have a wide foot," I said.

"Oh." The redhead stole a glance at my boxy feet.

"Okay, so you get free shit and you get benefits, but how do you pay your rent? Do you live at home? What she's offering doesn't even cover my rent, let alone anything else."

"We all live together," the blonde said.

"The four of you? Like in a house?" I asked.

"No, duh. We share a studio."

"Fuck no, you're lying," I said. I was twenty-five years old. The hell I was going to have a roommate again, and for sure not three! And not in a fucking studio apartment!

"No we're not. It's perfect," the redhead said. "We share a wardrobe since we're all the same size." (Which I assumed was zero.)

"How does that even work? How can you have four beds in a studio?" I asked, imagining bunk beds to the ceiling.

The girls laughed. "We have two beds," the dark-haired

girl said. "We tend not to sleep in our apartment that much, y'know? A lot of us have boyfriends and we can stay there."

Yeah, that wasn't going to work for me. Ebeneezer's dad was an Evangelical minister. We were barely allowed to be alone after dark, so sleeping over was never going to happen. EVER. "What about groceries?" I asked. All four of them looked at me with blank expressions. "Food?" I clarified. "Do you eat?"

Finally the fourth spoke for the first time. "That's one of the benefits of working here, besides the lipstick. There are events we can go to every night. Book signings, art openings, fashion shows, that sort of thing. There are always appetizers and an open bar. If you're still hungry, some dumb guy will buy you dinner."

"I see," I said, nodding slowly, taking it all in. "So, what's the end goal here?"

"What do you mean?" the blonde asked.

"Well, right now you're all young and hot and you can get men to share their beds and buy you food. But what happens when you hit thirty?" (Yeah, I said thirty. I know! I apologize, thirty-year-olds. Now I wish I were as young as you. I was only twenty-five at the time, so thirty seemed like a lifetime away and it seemed so damn old.)

The redhead shrugged. "We'll get married," she said, as if she'd just snap her fingers and some dumb guy would buy her dinner and a ring. Oh wait, it probably would happen that easy for her.

"And what about your career? Don't you want to get out of the archives? Margaret said hardly anyone gets out."

The dark-haired girl wrinkled her brow (well, she tried to, but the Botox prevented it). "This is just temporary. I'm just here so I can meet a rich guy at one of these galas and then my *career* will be managing our household."

"Rich, *hot* guy," the blonde clarified.

"Of course," the redhead said.

"You want a career here? In this dump?" the dark-haired girl asked. "You'll end up like Margaret."

"But it's not like you have a lot of choice," the blonde said, eyeing me critically. "I mean, we could help you...I think."

"No thank you!" I said quickly. I had flashbacks to middle school when a bunch of bitches tried to help me be cool. I was never going to do that again! "I have a boyfriend." I could tell none of them believed me. "We'll get married soon."

"Of course you will," the blonde said with just a hint of sarcasm in her voice.

"I want to be a writer," I said. "I thought writers worked here."

"I don't know any writers," the redhead said. "But I slept with the publisher's son once. I bet he knows writers."

What the fuck was she suggesting? That I sleep with the publisher's son? I'd had enough. "Okay, ladies. Thanks so much for the pep talk. I feel much better now. I really appreciate your insight," I said. "Please tell Margaret this helped."

The girls click-clacked out of my personal space and went on the hunt for the free foundation spotted on eighteen.

I stayed in the archives for a few more weeks. Carla sent me out on interviews almost every day, but nothing was a good fit for me. There was the one human resources representative who asked me, "Where do you see yourself in five years?" Apparently you are not supposed to say, "In your job." I meant it as a compliment. I figured she was kicking ass and so she'd move up in the world and then I could have her job. I guess no one wants to hear that.

And then there was the time I got confused and went to interview with the same company twice. They liked me enough to pick my resume out of the slush pile twice, but not enough to remember me until halfway through the interview. "Wait. Didn't I meet you last week?" the guy asked.

"Yes." I smiled, because I thought this was a second interview. I mean, they didn't say that exactly, but I thought it was implied.

He said, "Why are you here again?"

Oh. *Not* a second interview. "Um, Carla said..." I couldn't finish the sentence, because yeah, why was I there? Carla once again did not give me the necessary details to make an educated response.

"Carla needs to get her shit straight," he griped. "We passed on you already." And then he stood up and walked out. No "goodbye," "sorry," or anything. Like he was the one more inconvenienced in that situation!

Oh, I can't forget the group interview where five of us were interviewed at the same time for the same job. That wasn't awkward at all, to be the last of the five to answer the question, "What is your greatest weakness?" It took everything I had not to say, "Pretty much what they all said, plus I'm weak when it comes to saying no to my boss."

There was another interview where I trekked across town on a fucking bus at high noon on the sweatiest July day ever only to be met by a room full of people. At first I thought it was another group interview situation and we were waiting for more to show up, because no one spoke. They all just stared at me while I gulped ice water and tried to casually fan out my damp cooter. Finally I broke the silence by saying, "Should we get started?"

That's when one said, "Oh, the job's been filled, but we were just really curious to meet someone from Kansas. Are you a farmer?"

Fuck you. In your ear. Twice.

I was beginning to think I was going to end up in the archives permanently or back in the good doctor's office. If I couldn't find a permanent job, I at least needed a better temp job. The lack of sunlight was wearing me down and my tiny bathroom couldn't hold any more free tubes of lipstick and concealer that I couldn't say no to.

I called Carla. "Get me out of here. I need to see the sky."

"They might never let you back in the doors again," Carla warned. "What if something great opens up?"

"It's okay. I'm not cut out for the glossy magazine world," I told her. "Especially not this magazine. They're never going to let me write for them. My feet are too big for the free shoes, I can't wear red lipstick, and I don't have strong enough opinions about moisturizers. Just get me a job where I can make money. I don't even care about writing anymore."

"Really?" Carla said. "Because I have a ton of places I can send you if that's true."

"It's true. What do you have?" I asked, completely deflated. I'd been in New York City for only a few months and already I was willing to sacrifice my dreams.

"How about this one? They need a temp to fill in for the assistant to the CEO of a startup."

"Okay."

"You have to wear a skirt or dress every day and no bare legs."

"It's a startup! Aren't those the guys who wear hoodies and sneakers?"

"Yeah, well, it looks like they like their ladies to dress like ladies."

"Oh, for fuck's sake," I groaned.

"You get free lunch every day," she said.

"I'm in," I said, because do you know how much lunch costs in Manhattan? More than the new pantyhose I was going to have to buy.

# CHAPTER 6

## AND THEN DOROTHY WENT
## TO WORK FOR MARY POPPINS

"COME ON, CARLA," I said. "I know you've got something else for me." It was my third call to Carla in a week. I'd been temping all over Manhattan for more than a month, and I couldn't find anything I liked well enough to stay on. But I needed to see a dentist, and I didn't get dental insurance as a temp. I needed something permanent. At least long enough to get a cleaning and a filling.

"Again?" Carla asked. "You just left the startup."

"I had to," I replied. "The corporate culture was toddlers-meet-frat-house. They probably owned stock in red Solo cups."

"But they had free lunch!" Carla said.

"Yeah, you know how they let me know my free lunch was there, Carla? My boss would say, 'Bro, lunch is here.' Those guys called me 'bro' way too much, which is ironic when they insisted that I wear skirts and pantyhose every fucking day."

"Jen, you're like the Goldilocks of temp jobs. You always have a reason why you hate them all," Carla said, clearly exasperated.

"Not true," I argued. "This one isn't so bad, but I can tell they like me. They want to hire me and I just can't see myself answering phones for an insurance company for the rest of my life. I'm not equipped to be this fucking perky all the time."

"Are you sure you don't want to stay? They think you're great. You're the only temp I've sent them who can handle six phones at once."

"You pick up and say, 'Thank you for calling. Hold, please' and then actually put them on hold, not hang up on them. It's not rocket science."

"You'd be surprised how difficult that can be for some." Carla sighed.

"Help me, Carla," I whined.

"What about that last place? What was wrong with it?" I snorted. "I told you, they never talked. Everyone communicated through interoffice memos. It was so weird. I think they're all pod people. I was just there so they could eat my brain or something. But it probably lost all of its nutrition when it got too dumb from the work they made me do."

Carla laughed. "And the boob-sweat place?"

"Carla, I think the name speaks for itself. They never turned on their AC. It's fucking August in New York City. I chafed. I should get workmen's comp or something."

"Okay, what about the data-entry job I hooked you up with? That shit is mindless."

"Precisely. Mind. Less. Eight hours of data entry is my own personal hell."

"And then you were too precious to commute farther than an hour," Carla reminded me.

"I'm coming from Queens. It's already a thirty-minute haul into the city and then you wanted me to transfer to a bus and then walk fourteen blocks. I'd have to leave at dawn to be there on time. Plus, more chafing."

"Well, the good news for you is I got a new full-time opening today. And I think you're perfect for it."

I sighed heavily. Carla thought I was perfect for data entry and receptionist too. I was beginning to think Carla didn't even know me. "What is it? Do I have to be able to lift twenty pounds?"

"No, no, you're totally unqualified for manual labor, Jen," she said. Huh. Maybe she did know me. "No, this is an office job. A legit company. You'd be working on the executive floor."

My ears perked up. Executive floor. That sounded promising. That usually meant free food and whatever swag the executives didn't take home to their kids. If nothing else there would be AC—the executives would never let their balls sweat. "Go on," I said.

"The commute is twenty-five minutes, door to door."

"Love it."

"They speak to one another, or at least they spoke to me today on the phone."

"Perfect."

"And there's no data entry."

"Sold!"

"You'll work with the managing partner, plan the meetings, help him with presentations, that sort of thing. The benefits and the perks are phenomenal."

"Hmm," I said skeptically. "But do I get free lipstick?"

"No, you get actual benefits and perks. Weren't you just complaining the other day that your tooth hurt?"

"Yes."

"Yeah, you get that plus paid time off to volunteer every month and free Metro cards."

She told me the salary and I got excited. It was the first job that actually paid me more than temping. "What's the catch?" I asked.

"I don't know. My guess is the boss is demanding, the work is hard. Something like that. Who knows? You won't know until you get there."

"Can I temp first and see what I think?"

"No. This one wants to hire someone and get them to work right away."

"Okay," I said.

"Great. You need to be there for an interview in an hour," Carla said.

"An hour?" I said. "I'm not ready! I've done no research. I know nothing about the company. I'm going to bomb this."

"You're going to be fine. We need to move fast, because everyone's going to send over their rock star. You've gone to dozens of interviews. You know all the questions. You're a seasoned pro. I'm sending you the address now. Good luck." I went to hang up when I heard Carla say, "Jen!"

I put the receiver back up to my ear. "Yeah?"

"This one is a good one, Jen. Don't fuck it up, or I'll put you in a mailroom next."

———

An hour later I was sinking into the softest, leatheriest couch ever. A young woman handed me a glass of ice water. In a real glass. Not one of those paper cone cups that every other office had provided me with. That shit was crystal.

"Good luck," she whispered.

The door opened and Philip Jenkins entered. Carla had told me he was British, but she didn't need to—the guy just oozed adorable, old man British-ness. His dapper suit fit him perfectly and I half expected to see a pocket watch peeking out at me. His tie and his socks were loud, but in a quirky, fashionable way—the girls back in the fashion magazine archives would approve. With his neat hair and his spectacles (Philip would never call them "glasses") perched precariously on his nose, he was practically perfect in every way. Like a male Mary Poppins.

"Good afternoon, Miss Mann," he said, peering at me over his specs. "Are you comfortable? Do you have plenty to drink?"

"Yes, I'm fine. Thank you," I replied. I was thirsty, but I was afraid if I drank too much then I'd need a restroom in the middle of the interview. I didn't want to do anything to mess up this opportunity. I could tell that Carla was getting sick of me, and even I was getting sick of me. It was time to settle down and maybe Carleton Corporation would be the place to settle.

"Wonderful. Shall we start?" he asked, sitting down at his large wooden desk.

"Yes, please," I replied, in an awful British accent. I refrained from clapping my hand over my mouth, but I did pinch my arm. *What the fuck, Jen? Stop that!* my brain yelled.

I have this problem where I mimic British or southern accents as soon as I hear them. It's so stupid, but I can't help myself—I just naturally fall into their speech patterns. The problem is my impressions are horrible. As in, I sound like a bad American actress trying to play an Australian trying to play a Cockney cabdriver trying to play Queen Elizabeth. My accent is so bad that the person I'm imitating always assumes I'm making fun of them. I'm not trying to be a jerk

—I just can't control myself or do a better accent. It's shite. See? Even my swears become Britishy when I'm writing about my inability to stop mimicking Brits. I checked Philip's reaction, but if he noticed, he was too polite to let me know.

"Brilliant," he said, launching into a long-winded explanation of the job I was interviewing for (he did sound a bit demanding, and the job did sound a little hard, something about managing the partner meetings and stuff like that, but I was up for the challenge) and then he dove into his own history and how he ended up in America (something to do with meeting a beautiful American socialite on holiday in "Ibitha," falling in love, and then following her to New York City where he married her, as one does) and then finally he asked me, "Tell me, Jen, why do you want this job? Why do you want to work for Carleton Corporation?" "Umm... Uhh..." *Shit.* Over the last few weeks Carla and I had gone over a myriad of possible interview questions, but this one had not come up. I was on my own. I was going to have to pull something out of my ass. "I, uh, well, uh, I mean, of course, Carleton Corporation is a very reputable company in their ... uh ... field," I said. I hadn't had time to do my research, so I didn't know what their "field" was exactly and I hoped the reputable part was true.

Philip nodded solemnly. "One of the finest."

"And, uh, well, I wanted to do something with my college degree. I have a degree in English and I want to be able to write and I was told there was a lot of writing, um, with, uh, this job here at, you know, Carleton." God, I sounded like a terrible writer!

"There is, indeed. I will require your expertise daily," Philip said.

"And, so, um, I just want to be vital, y'know?"

Philip nodded again. "Oh, I *do* know," he said. "Don't we all? There is nothing better than devoting your life to a company that cares about you the way Carleton cares about their employees. Carleton values their employees and really makes you feel like you're adding to the success. I'm just so lucky to be here."

I nodded silently. Carleton Corporation sounded like it was either amazing or it was a cult.

Philip shifted gears. "Now, let me ask you about Kansas."

I tried not to groan. I was so tired of people asking me about Kansas. Apparently I needed a job with the Kansas Tourism Office! "Um, okay, what about it?"

"What is Kansas like?"

I thought for a moment. Most people I'd encountered in New York City only knew about Kansas from *The Wizard of Oz*. It was weird how many of them really thought Kansas was still stuck in the Dust Bowl, where houses were picked up by twisters and dropped on witches daily. "It's very vast," I said. "I lived in the city—well, the suburbs, actually—but not on a farm. There is a lot of countryside outside the city limits, but I don't know anyone who lives there. There are lots of farms, but many of them are commercial farms, huge operations."

"Hardworking people?" Philip inquired.

I shrugged. "Sure, I guess. Some of them."

"What about you? Have you lived in the Midwest a long time? I see you went to college in Iowa."

I shrugged again. "Yeah, I've spent a lot of my life in the Midwest." I was concerned. I didn't want Philip to think I was some kind of country bumpkin. I needed to make it clear that I was very metropolitan too. "I lived in New Jersey when I was a kid." Jersey was cosmopolitan, right?

I saw Philip frown ever so slightly. New Jersey was not impressing him. "You see, Megan—you met her, she's the one who brought your drink—Megan has been with me for many years now. It is her job that I am looking to fill. She's leaving me." Philip smiled sadly.

"Where is she going?" I asked.

"She was promoted within."

"Oh, that's good," I said. Real good. This was the first job I'd interviewed for where I wasn't replacing someone who had been fired and escorted from the building by security.

"Yes, it's lovely for her, but it's terrible for me," Philip said. "Anyway, Megan is a hardworking Midwestern girl. She's from Minnesota. That's very near to Kansas, yes?"

"Umm." I didn't have the heart to tell him that I'd have to drive all the way across Iowa to get to Minnesota. New Yorkers get the Midwest confused. Geography is not their thing. They think Iowa, Idaho, and Ohio are all the same state. In their minds anything west of Jersey and east of Vegas is all one state filled with farmland and hardworking people who are probably related to one another due to inbreeding. So I said, "Sure, sure. I've been there." It wasn't a total lie.

"Megan has been incredible. She gets here on time, she stays late when I need her to, she's professional and, um..." Philip groped for the right word.

"Hardworking?" I asked, since that seemed to be his favorite word.

"Yes! Precisely! And I believe I owe it all to her Midwestern upbringing. You Midwesterners have work ethic for days! That's what I want. To be honest, your resume was fine. It wasn't spectacular, it didn't do much for me. It was just fine. But! When I saw you were from Kentucky, I said to myself, 'She is the Midwestern girl for me.'"

I didn't even correct him that Kentucky and Kansas aren't the same, nor is Kentucky considered the Midwest. I just nodded. "So, you're interviewing me for this job mostly because I'm from the Midwest?" I asked.

Philip nodded vigorously. "Yes, yes, I am."

"Wow," I said. "That seems kind of crazy, right?"

"No, not at all. In fact," Philip said, "I'm *offering* you the job because you're from the Midwest. I don't need to see anyone else. All of the other applicants are local, and now that I've met you I want you to take Megan's spot."

I looked around. The AC was pumping. The ice in my crystal water glass hadn't even begun to melt. Philip could clearly speak and wasn't going to communicate with me via interoffice memos. The job did not sound mindless. In fact, it sounded really interesting. And the perks and benefits were actually something to brag about. I didn't really care that I was being offered a job by a guy who didn't know the difference between Kansas and Kentucky—I couldn't tell you the name of another English city besides London. I kind of liked the fact that he thought all Midwesterners were hardworking, but to be honest, I was a little worried I might not be able to live up to those expectations since I wasn't really known for my work ethic but more for my napping abilities. I decided to ignore all of my concerns and focus on the positive: free Metro cards instead of free lipstick.

"Well, then, I accept," I said. "Brilliant!"

Philip had been looking at something on his desk and his head snapped up. He might have missed my terrible

British accent the first time, but he definitely heard it this time.

I fought to keep my face neutral and innocent. I said, "Oops. Sometimes my unusual Midwestern accent slips out. I need to work on that."

"Indeed," Philip sniffed.

# CHAPTER 7

## I DO NOT GET PAID ENOUGH FOR THIS SHIT

I HAD PLANNED and attended several partner meetings for Carleton Corporation, but the one in Palm Springs was my first major off-site event. We were hosting all of the partners and their families at an exclusive resort. Philip and I had been working nonstop for months to get this event planned, and my strong Midwestern work ethic was being tested on all levels. We'd been sequestered in a boardroom that was serving as our War Room for a few days and all of the support staff was on edge. I was plotting out the seating chart for the evening's meal with a world-renowned chef when my cell rang.

"Hi, Jen. This is Lucien, from Mike's office," the voice on the other end of the phone said.

"Lucien?" I asked, flipping through my mental Rolodex and coming up blank. "I'm going to need some more info." I only had a thousand other details running through my head at that moment.

"Yes, sorry. I'm Mike's newest assistant."

"Oh, hi. Where's Dom?" I asked. Dom was my usual contact in Mike's office.

"It didn't work out," Lucien said, a little too gleefully.

*Of course it didn't,* I thought. Mike was a partner that I didn't work with very often. He didn't come to many of the meetings, he usually phoned in from a private island or a Swiss chalet. I didn't know him well but the rumor around the water cooler was he liked to surround himself with young, good-looking assistants with limited job security. I wasn't sure if he fired them because he grew bored with them or if they actually did something wrong. Either way, Lucien was the third or fourth I'd dealt with, but Dom had been around the longest. I'd just spoken to him the Monday before. Mike didn't mess around!

"Okay, well, congratulations," I said. "What can I do for you?"

"Mike has to leave early today," Lucien said breathlessly. "He just decided fifteen minutes ago. Of course he did, right? It's only my second day, why go easy on me! Anyway, the pilots are on their way to the plane. He wants to be wheels-up in less than a hour."

"All right, well, I'll let the Chairman know," I said.

We were holding the meeting at this particular resort because Carleton Corporation had recently acquired a new company. The resort was close to the company's headquarters and there were several events scheduled for later that morning. The Chairman was excited for the group to see it all. I'd arranged for a tour of the entire facility, brief meetings with the heads of departments, a beautiful luncheon back at the resort overlooking the golf course and then leisure activities for the entire family in the afternoon. The meetings and events I planned always sounded amazing, but I never actually got to participate. I spent the entire time closed off in a windowless boardroom in the hotel where I was taking care of everyone's tiniest whim and desire. For instance, the Chairman only drank Pellegrino at room temperature. His minibar needed to be cleared out in advance, unplugged, and refilled with Pellegrino, labels facing slightly to the right. Whereas Mr. Wang only drank Fiji water chilled to thirty-eight degrees. Mrs. Dennis always needed a suite, no mater if the meetings lasted one night or one week. The suite had to be on a high floor and replenished with fresh flowers every day—but NO TULIPS (her assistant's note was in all caps like Mrs. Dennis had a deadly allergy to tulips or something). Mr. Smith was the candy guy. He needed Snickers, Hershey bars, and bowls of green M&Ms at arm's length from the bed, the couch, and the desk, but not *on* the desk; the desk was for working. It was a lot to remember, so I had an entire binder for each partner detailing their (and some spouses') demands. When a person joined the partnership, their office was sent a multi-page questionnaire where we asked them to list all their needs and wants right down to sheet thread count and preferred size and heft of towels. Sometimes I thought the assistants were just fucking with me. Did Mrs. Klein really need half a gallon of goat milk every single day? I highly doubted it, but I wasn't about to call her bluff and not arrange for the goat milk.

In the scheme of things, Mike was actually one of my more low-key partners—just the fact that I could call him Mike was a rarity. None of the other partners encouraged me to use their first names, nor did they ever ask mine. It was just, "Excuse me? You there, yes you, I need canned oxygen after my cryotherapy treatment at four. Make sure there's plenty in my room." I'm not saying Mike was low-maintenance though. The guy was a legit billionaire, so of course he had some demands. He always wanted a suite and he had some specific drink and food requests, but nothing had to face a certain direction or be a certain temperature and he never banned certain colors. The Chairman wouldn't be thrilled that Mike was leaving early, but there was nothing he could do. Mike always came and went as he pleased and he never stayed around for the "fun" stuff. He never had me plan excursions for him. Mike was all business all the time. I guess that's why he was a billionaire and I wasn't.

"Great," Lucien said. "I didn't want to call the Chairman. I don't have the time."

"Oh my God!" I exclaimed. "Lucien, you can *never* call the Chairman!"

"Really? Because his cell is programmed into the phone Mike gave me. It was Dom's phone."

"You might have the number, but you shouldn't. Mike should never have given it to you. And you can *never* call the Chairman. Like, *ever*. If it's related to partner meetings and events it goes through me, otherwise you must call Cynthia, the Chairman's first assistant. She would have your head if you called him directly. Shit, she'd have your head if you called his third assistant. Cynthia is the gatekeeper. She holds the power. Don't go around her."

"That's a lot to remember," Lucien said.

"Don't you have a binder? Every executive assistant I know has a binder. You need a binder!"

"I'm not an executive assistant. I'm a special assistant," Lucien said haughtily.

I didn't even want to know what that meant, but I did know he needed a fucking binder. "Look, Lucien. I'm just saying, there's a protocol. Like a hierarchy, or whatever. You can't overstep your bounds. You can't call him directly. The Chairman wouldn't know what to do if you called him up on his private cell phone. He barely knows my name and I sort of work for the man, so he sure as shit doesn't know yours. If Cynthia didn't have you killed, the Chairman would probably crush your soul and have you fired. Maybe that's what Dom did? Maybe he called the Chairman? We are peons. We are here to do their bidding."

"Speaking of doing their bidding, being peons, et cetera," Lucien said, "that's really why I'm calling. Mike needs your help."

"Of course," I said, thinking I'd need to arrange a car or a helicopter to get him to his plane. "What do you need?" I grabbed Mike's binder so I could find his preferred limo company and car color. I prayed it was black, because odd colors were hard to find on short notice.

"I need you to go to his suite and pack his luggage."

"What?" I asked, practically dropping my binder.

"Normally his pilots do it, but like I said, Mike wants to be wheels-up in less than an hour and they need to get through their pre-flight check. They don't have time to pack or they'll be late taking off. You just need to put his stuff in his bag and I've got a car coming in fifteen minutes to pick it up and take it to the jet."

"Um," I said. "Okay." Carleton Corporation had asked me to do a number of odd things over the years, but pack someone's luggage was a new one.

"Call me when you get to his suite and I'll walk you through his packing list so you can be sure you've got it all."

"Right. Of course. I'm on my way."

I grabbed the extra room key and dashed out of the conference room. I was momentarily blinded by the sunlight. "Ahh!" I said. *When was the last time I saw the sun?* Definitely not yesterday, since I was in the War Room before dawn and ended up falling asleep on the floor while I waited for Philip to come back from dinner so we could finalize the seating chart for breakfast. Maybe the day before?

By the time I drove a golf cart across the resort, caught the elevator to the top floor of Mike's building, and walked what seemed like half a mile to Mike's suite (because low-maintenance Mike didn't like to be near the elevators—too noisy), my phone was ringing again.

"Jen? Are you there? Car's ETA is eight minutes," Lucien said.

"I'm doing the best I can, Lucien. This resort is massive and I have very stumpy legs." I swiped the key card and entered Mike's spacious suite. It was so different from the double room on the second floor I was sharing with my coworker Tanya.

"Mike wants to know where his bag is," Lucien hissed in my ear. "He's calling my other phone."

"He's going to have to wait," I snapped. "I'm doing the best I can!" *Fuck!* And I thought my boss was demanding! For such a low-maintenance dude, Mike was becoming a real pain in my ass.

"There's a navy suit in the closet," Lucien said to me. I heard him apologize on his other phone to Mike for my ineptitude, "She's slow in more than one way, if you know what I mean, Mike."

"Got the suit," I said, grabbing the suit, the two shirts, and the sweater from the closet before I was asked. *I might be slow, but I can fucking pack a bag!* I tossed them into Mike's leather suitcase. "What else?"

"Four pairs of socks in the top drawer, four undershirts in the middle drawer, and a bathrobe on the back of the bathroom door."

"How do you know where everything is, Lucien?" I asked, grabbing the bathrobe.

"The pilots unpack him and they follow Mike's chart. He's very specific. Everywhere he goes is the same setup."

"Of course," I said, grabbing the toiletries bag from the counter.

Lucien kept barking orders at me and I kept tossing stuff into the suitcase.

"Bottom drawer should have four pairs of underwear," Lucien said.

I opened the bottom drawer. "There are three, but whatever," I said, snatching them and tossing them into the suitcase. I spotted Mike's pajamas and workout gear thrown over a chair and I took those too before I was prompted.

"Wait. Did you just say there are only three pairs of underwear?" Lucien said, a bit panicky.

"Yeah," I said, throwing the books on the bedside table into the suitcase.

"Stop moving!" Lucien demanded. "I need to think."

"What?" I said.

"I can't think with you breathing heavily in my ear! Stop moving! A pair of underwear is missing, Jen. Every night Mike sends his dirty clothes to the hotel laundry. I have that inventory and there is no underwear on the list. We're missing a pair of underwear. Do you see it anywhere?"

"A pair of underwear?" I asked.

"Check the bathroom," Lucien said.

I looked around the cavernous bathroom but couldn't see the tighty whities anywhere. "They're not here," I said.

"Hang on," Lucien said, irritated. I could hear him mumbling into his other phone.

"Oh my God, Lucien, who cares if there's a pair of underwear missing? Is Mike really getting his knickers in a twist over this?" I was highly offended when Lucien didn't laugh at my excellent underwear joke.

"Okay, crisis averted," Lucien said, coming back on the line with me. "Mike says they're behind the bathroom door."

I slowly closed the bathroom door and, sure enough, I spotted a wad of fabric tucked into a corner. It was Mike's dirty drawers. "Oh," I gasped.

"You see them?" Lucien said, relief flooding his voice. He spoke into his other phone, "We've got them, Mike."

"I—uh—yeah, I see them, but..."

"But what?" Lucien said. "The car is ETA two minutes. You need to *move*, Jen! Grab them and go!"

"Grab them?" I said, eyeing the soiled skivvies.

"Yes!"

"Grab them with my hand?" I asked, giving the putrid panties a push with my toe.

"What the fuck else would you use?" Lucien said.

"It's just that they're dirty, Lucien. They're a pair of men's dirty underwear and you want me to grab them with my bare hand."

"They're Mike's," Lucien said, as if that made it all better. As if a billionaire's ass crack didn't smell as bad as a poor man's. As if a billionaire's ball sweat was easier to handle than a middle-class man's ball sweat. As if a billionaire's skid marks were less revolting than a millionaire's skid marks.

At that moment my cell's call waiting beeped. It was my boss. "Hang on, Lucien, Philip is trying to reach me."

"You *cannot* hang up until I know you've got Mike's bag fully packed," Lucien barked.

"Philip has no idea where I went. I can't ignore him. Just hang on a second."

"No, Jen," Lucien said firmly. "Mike outranks Philip. Philip's just an EVP. You're the one preaching at me about office protocol."

"Your boss's nut hut doesn't outrank my boss!" I said, pushing the button. "Hey, Philip, listen, I'm in Mike's suite."

Philip's voice sounded surprised. "What exactly are you doing there, Jen?"

"Long story short, Mike is leaving early, his new assistant is having a cow and wants me to pack up Mike's things because he can't do it himself and the pilots don't have time and right now I'm in the bathroom staring at Mike's dirty underwear and wondering what I did to get here. Philip, Mike wants me to touch them. He wants me to put them in his suitcase. The man is a billionaire! Can't he buy a new pair? Can't he bill Carleton for a new pair? I mean, come on, Philip! You don't pay me enough for this!"

Philip let out a heavy sigh. "No, we certainly don't. Is everything else packed?"

"Yes."

"Fine. I'm on my way."

"On your way? Here?" I asked.

"Yes, bring down the suitcase. I shall get Mike's undergarments." I could practically hear Philip's spine go straighter as he dug down into his British resolve. Midwesterners might be hard workers, but the British are steely.

I hung up and got Lucien on the line again. "Philip's on his way to deal with Mike's underthings," I said.

"The car is waiting," Lucien said, practically crying. "I don't know what's worse—to be late or not have the goddamn underwear."

"This is a real thing you're worried about, Lucien?" I asked.

"Yes! Yes, it is!" Lucien snapped. "I'm sorry that you are not important enough to worry about this sort of thing, but I am. This is the kind of shit Dom got fired over. I will not be fired because you're afraid to touch a pair of fucking underwear!"

"This is ridiculous, Lucien. I'm taking the suitcase down now. You can have Mike call me if he has a problem with his missing panties."

I lugged Mike's suitcase to the lobby. It didn't have wheels. Of course it didn't, probably because Mike had never carried it himself and never realized what a solid leather suitcase actually weighed empty, let alone full. The driver helped me wrestle the bag into the car and he assured me that the suitcase would arrive long before Mike, especially since he wasn't supposed to pick him up from the tennis courts for another hour. So much for wheels-up in less than an hour.

On Monday morning I arrived at work and found a plastic bag on my desk. It was one of those plastic bags the hotels give you. I think you're supposed to use them to send out your laundry, but I always use them to cart home wet swimsuits. The name of the resort where we'd stayed was stamped on the front and inside was Mike's (freshly washed) underwear and a note: *Please FedEx this package overnight to Mike with my deepest apologies –Philip.*

Carleton might not have paid me enough to touch dirty drawers, but I guess they paid Philip enough.

## CHAPTER 8

### YOU CAN'T FIRE ME—I QUIT!

I HAD BEEN WORKING for Philip and Carleton Corporation for about two years when he fired me with a Post-it Note.

It came as a huge surprise, because I thought we were getting along great. We had split our duties fairly evenly—I did all of the grunt work and he took all of the credit and earned about ten times what I did. We both traveled to beautiful and exotic locales with the partners. The only sightseeing I got to do was to and from the airport. I gulped down cold room service and never got to see anything outside of the hotel conference rooms. He ate with celebrity chefs and went golfing with the executives. He did bail me out, though, when I refused to pick up Mike's grubby grapeslinger and I will always be indebted to him for that.

It all happened during the dreaded quarterly review period. Once a quarter our company made us sit down and take a long, hard look at ourselves and our jobs. We had to examine everything we did and basically plead our case as to why we were still a vital cog in Carleton Corporation's giant wheel. We had to explain what our current job was and what our goals were for the upcoming quarter. How we'd increase revenue and bring down costs. This was the trickiest part for me. I had to think outside the box and try to come up with new jobs for myself. I was an executive assistant—there wasn't much more I could do. I answered phones, wrote correspondence and speeches, I planned meetings, I filed, I made copies, and I fetched coffee. Technically, I added nothing to the bottom line of the company. I was pure overhead. I couldn't exactly promise to bring in millions of dollars in new revenue or cut costs in any significant way. I could offer to spend less on Post-it Notes, but I really liked my Post-its. It was so nice not to have to get three signatures just to get Post-its, and I admit I took advantage—I got the fancy pop-up ones.

So, I'd pull fifty-cent words out of my ass that sounded great and make my goals a lot of fluff and very little substance. I put a lot in there about working beyond my potential and pushing myself to accomplish more than just my basic job requirements and blah, blah, blah. I would always spin it that without me the board couldn't run as efficiently as it did or some shit like that. It was my eighth time filling out the stupid thing and it took some serious brainpower and word wizardry to come up with new bullshit. I put that creative writing degree to the fucking test and finally finished the review just before my lunch break. I dropped it on Philip's desk on my way out the door.

When I came back a half hour later, I could see my review was back on my desk. It had one of my giant yellow Post-it Notes plastered in the middle. (Yeah, I got the big ones too. I have a real problem with Post-its, okay?) I could see words scrawled across the note in Philip's neat block letters, written in red Blood Pen (I got Philip hooked on those pens soon after I was hired). *Uh-oh,* I thought. *That doesn't look good.* I didn't think it was anything terrible, but I figured that Philip had some edits he wanted made before he sent my review over to the Chairman's office. He was kind of a micromanager in that regard. I wasn't so much worried about being in trouble as I was irritated that I was going to have to work on it some more and pull more bull-shit out of my ass.

I plopped down at my desk and grabbed the paper. A giant red X was drawn through my entire review and the Post-it Note read:

*JEN HAS NO FUTURE GOALS AS HER JOB WILL BE ELIMINATED IN APPROXIMATELY 7 MONTHS.*

Philip's signature was scrawled across the bottom.
*Wait. What the actual fuck??*
I read the note about a hundred more times, because what the fuck was happening?

I stormed over to Philip's office. His door was closed and I had been instructed to never interrupt him when his door was closed, but fuck that noise. I knocked boldly on the door. No answer. I knocked again. "Philip?"

Finally he answered. "Come in, Jen."

I opened the door and found Philip lying on his couch. I'd never seen Philip even sit on his couch, let alone *lie* on it.

"Oh my God, are you okay?" I asked, forgetting the Post-it Note immediately and suddenly concerned about his well-being. Maybe he was having a brain aneurysm and that was why he wrote what he wrote?

Philip sat up. "Yes, I'm fine, thank you."

Oh. So, no aneurysm. "Okay, good," I said. "Listen, I got your...er, note."

Philip had the decency to blush a little. "Oh, uh, very good."

"No, not very good. What the fuck, Philip?" I said.

Philip looked downright alarmed. Up until that point, I'd always been very professional with Philip. I cussed with Tanya and held nothing back with my friends at lunch, but the most impolite thing Philip had ever heard me say was, "Excuse me?" instead of "Pardon me?" And when I said that we'd had a five-minute discussion about how Philip thought "excuse me" was crass. I didn't care though. I could not filter myself any longer. This was bullshit.

He held up his hands in surrender. "It's not personal, Jen," he said. "It's just business."

"Business?"

"Yes, the company has been acquired and your job is redundant."

"Redundant?"

"Yes, that means—"

"I know what that means, Philip! I'm just trying to process here. How come this is the first I've heard of it? It was never in the notes I typed up from the meetings and stuff."

"Yes, I know. I typed those notes myself," Philip said. "We needed absolute discretion on this one."

So *I'm redundant* and *untrustworthy?* I thought. Actually, I am terrible with secrets, so it was probably best he didn't tell me. "When is this all happening?" I asked.

"The transition period will be the next five or six months, but we won't tell the employees for four, probably. Maybe even five. However, I wanted to let you know so that you can help us transition better."

"What do you mean?"

"Well, there's going to be a lot that you'll have to show

your replacement...er, counterpart. You'll have to train this person so they'll know how to do your job."

"I thought my job was redundant. Doesn't this person know how to do my job?" "Well, there is someone who manages the parent-company meetings, but now she'll need to know your systems and protocols. Many of our employees will need to do this, actually. They just won't understand fully *why* they're doing that."

"Wait. You're not going to tell them?" I was horrified.

"We find that if we tell people their jobs are being eliminated, they tend not to work very hard in those final days," Philip said with complete sincerity and not a hint of realization that what he was describing was a total dick move.

"What about Tanya?" I asked.

"Oh yes, Tanya will have to go," Philip said. "But don't tell her, Jen. No one can know. You're the first on the floor to know, well, except Cynthia."

"Is she going?"

"No, of course not. She's necessary."

"But I'm not," I said.

"You're taking it personally again, Jen. Don't do that, please. Now, the Chairman and I are trusting you with this information. Many, many, many of our employees are redundant. And then, of course, there will be the businesses that we must sell off. It will be up to the new owners to decide what to do with them when that time comes. But no one can know yet. It will upset a great deal of people."

"Naturally," I said. I frowned. "What about you, Philip? Where are you going? Can't I go with you?"

Philip chortled at the very idea. "Oh no, Jen!" he said. "I've accepted the buyout."

"Buyout?" I asked.

"Yes, they've made me an offer I can't refuse. Clarice and I will be retiring to the South of France."

"Shit! That's not a buyout, that's a golden parachute," I said.

Philip blushed again. "Don't forget, Jen, I've put in many years here," he said. The "I'm owed" part was silent.

"So that's it, then?" I said. "I'm just out?"

"Well not today, of course, Jen. Don't be so dramatic. You have five to seven months or so. You're very important to the organization, Jen. We value you—highly," Philip said.

"Really? Because it doesn't feel like it, Philip. You fired me with a Post-it Note. You didn't even bring me in to talk about it. You just wrote it on a piece of paper and left it on my desk."

"You're not being fired, Jen. You're redundant. There is a difference. I'll write you a recommendation, of course." I could feel the icy waves of panic overwhelming me. Five months—seven, tops—and I'd be out of a job. The weight of my bills piled on me. Shit, I'd just bought new fancy fucking shoes last week! I was wearing them, so I couldn't even return them. Why hadn't Philip given me the Post-it Note last week and then I would have never bought the shoes! Actually, that wasn't true. I shop and eat when I'm depressed, so I probably would have still bought the shoes, but they would have been an I'm-so-sad-I-lost-my-job purchase rather than a go-me-I'm-killing-it-at-my-job-and-I-deserve-fancy-shoes purchase. *Blergh.* "I need to make a call," I said.

Philip looked alarmed. "You look ill, Jen. Are you all right? Do you need to go down to the clinic?"

I waved him off. "No, no, I'm fine. This is just kind of a big shock for me, that's all. I live paycheck to paycheck, Philip. I know that's probably hard for you to understand."

Philip looked perplexed. Of course he did. I was privy to all of Philip's bills. Just the week before he'd spent ten grand on trees for his beach house. Trees! When the bill came across my desk, I was certain there was a mistake.

I had called him on the speakerphone. "Hey, Philip, I think we have a problem. Some landscaper faxed over a bill for ten thousand dollars for trees for the beach house. This can't be right."

"Which beach house?" he asked. "Southampton or Jupiter?"

I'd completely forgotten about his Florida beach house. "Hamptons."

"Oh, then yes, that's fine. I had some lovely spruces transplanted. Seven of them."

I choked on my tea. "This bill is only for seven trees?" I sputtered.

"They were transplanted, Jen. From a hundred-year-old forest. That's actually quite reasonable."

"I see. So pay it, then?"

"Yes, please."

It wasn't just trees he spent money on. Every day he took a private town car from his McMansion in Connecticut to the office. One time he asked me where I lived. "Do you live in Manhattan, Jen?"

"No, I'm out in Queens."

"Ah, Queens. That's where the airport is."

"Yes, I live very close to LaGuardia."

"That must be...er...convenient for you," he said.

"Very. Also, it's loud." Not only did I live in the flight path for LaGuardia, I also lived a block from what I could only assume was the busiest fire station in all five boroughs.

"How is your commute to work?"

"It's not too bad," I said. "I live on an express line, so it's just a few stops."

"Express line," Philip said. "That's a subway, then?"

"Yes, I take the subway every day."

"How exciting," he said.

I frowned. "Kind of. I've been flashed several times. And twice, drunk men have peed in the corners of my train car."

"Oh my God! Really?"

"Really. People are animals, Philip."

"Well, why do you do it, then?"

"Do what? Ride the subway?" I was totally confused.

"Yes."

"I have to get to work, Philip," I chuckled. "I can't take a town car every day."

"It's quite comfortable," Philip said. "And you can get so much work done on the ride. It would be nice to have a dedicated driver, but that's an expense I just can't justify."

"And that's how I feel about a town car."

On my birthday, Philip always sent me a gorgeous, elaborate flower arrangement from the florist at the Waldorf Astoria. The first year, I received it on a Friday. My first thought was, *Thanks, but how the hell am I supposed to get these home?* I didn't want to leave the flowers in the office over the weekend because I was sure they'd die. I spent the rest of the day trying to figure out how I could carry such an enormous flower arrangement onto the crowded subway with me. In the end, I went out for celebratory drinks with my friends and then hauled that shit home on the subway later that night when it wasn't so busy and I could get a seat. It was so heavy and awkward to carry, but at least it blocked my view of the pervert wagging his peen at me. *If he comes any closer,*

*I'm smashing this vase over his head,* I thought. By the time I got home, half of the water had sloshed out of the vase and onto me and the bulk of the flowers were mangled. I should have just left the damn thing to die at the office.

When Philip handed me the bill to pay the following week, I was stunned to see he had paid two hundred dollars for the flowers. "Why didn't he just give me cash?" I muttered, writing the check.

Sometimes the other assistants and I would talk about how we felt a little bit like zoo animals. Our über-wealthy bosses had no idea how we lived. It wasn't like we lived badly. We weren't on welfare or public assistance of any kind. We lived in clean, safe neighborhoods. We just didn't live like they did. We didn't have memberships to fancy clubs or a beach house—or two. They had no idea that two hundred dollars would be such a better gift than flowers. But there was no way to tell them that.

I tried once. I think it was the third time Philip sent me flowers. "Hey Philip, thanks so much for the flowers," I said, motioning to the gorgeous display on my desk. "It really wasn't necessary."

Philip waved off my concerns. "Oh, it was fine. You deserved them. It's Secretary's Day and I wanted you to know that you are appreciated."

"Well, I appreciate the thought. I really do. It's just that..." I trailed off.

Philip frowned. "What is it? Are you allergic to flowers?"

"No, not at all. It's just that I see the bills for these and they're so expensive," I said.

Philip nodded. "They're excellent quality."

"They really are!" I agreed. "They're stunning. It's just

that...well, I mean, have you ever thought about maybe spending that money on something a bit more useful?"

"Useful? I don't understand."

"So, the flowers, they're really pretty and they smell great and everything, but they're dead within just a few days. They're not very useful."

"You think I'm wasting my money?" Philip asked.

"Maybe?" I said. "It seems like a lot of money for something that's going to die. We were talking—"

"Who was talking?" Philip asked.

"The other executive assistants and I. We were saying how it's great to get these flowers and everything, but it kind of seems wasteful for you bosses. You guys could use that money elsewhere, I bet." This is where I stopped talking because I was afraid I was overstepping. I didn't want Philip to think I was an asshole or something. I was hoping he'd read between the lines and next time he'd think, "I should get Jen a two-hundred-dollar gift card to Target instead of flowers."

I should not have stopped talking. I should have kept going because Philip did not understand what I was saying. Not even close. That year for Christmas I got an Hermès scarf. I don't know how Philip thought that was practical. But actually, looking back, it wasn't such a bad gift. I ended up eBaying that thing for two hundred and fifty bucks, so I guess it worked out.

"I hope you're not worried about your job security, Jen," Philip said, guiding me to sit beside him on the sofa.

"I have no job security now, Philip," I said.

"Well, you've got a job for several more months and don't forget your severance. You'll get a package to tide you over a bit."

"How much?" I asked.

"Everyone is different. For you, it will be one week's salary for every year you've worked here."

"I've worked here two years."

"Oh. Well, then," he said, adjusting his spectacles.

"Yeah."

The next day I received a beautiful floral arrangement from Philip.

# CHAPTER 9

## WATCH OUT, I'M A VERY
## DANGEROUS KOALA BEAR

THE WRITING WAS LITERALLY on the Post-it Note: I
needed to find a new job. Pronto. I called up Carla the
headhunter and told her I was dusting off my resume.

"Give me whatever you've got, Carla. I need a new job
right way." I couldn't tell her that soon almost every executive assistant at Carleton Corporation would be out of a job,
but I wanted to be ahead of the rush.

"That's actually terrific news, Jen," Carla said. "I just
had lunch yesterday with Paula. She's the head of HR at
XYZ Media. She's a total pain in the ass, but at least you
don't have to work for her, right? She has an amazing opportunity at XYZ."

"What's the job?" I asked.

"The usual. Executive assistant to the Chairman. He's
young though. Like thirty-five. His dad started XYZ and last
year handed it over to this guy and his brother. The brother
really runs the company. This guy, the Chairman, he's a
playboy. He jets around the world and attends parties. He's
the 'face' of XYZ. My guess is you'll do a lot of travel book-
ing, house management stuff. Pay's good and the benefits

are great, hours are light since he really doesn't 'do' much at the company. They need someone right away. I could get you in tomorrow."

I didn't even hesitate. "Sounds good. Let me know when it's set up."

"Do you need some flexibility? Maybe I could see if they have some free time during lunch?"

"Carla, I was let go via Post-it Note. These fuckers are lucky I didn't stomp out the door yesterday. I told them I'd stay here so I can help them transition, and I'll stay as long as they'll pay me—or until I find a new job, whichever comes first. They have no loyalty to me and so I have none to them. I need a job, so I'm going to interview whenever I damn well please. I dare Philip to try and stop me. Set it up and I'll be there."

"Look at you, ballsy!" Carla said. "Where's the quiet, hardworking Midwestern girl I met a couple of years ago?"

"I think they sent her out to buy more Post-it Notes."

I went home that night and read everything I could about XYZ Media. Even though the job really didn't entail getting into the nitty-gritty of XYZ, I still wanted to be well versed on what they did so I could speak intelligently during my interview the next day. I found out that the man I would work for was indeed thirty-five and a playboy. He was the stereotypical rich boy who became a big shot because his daddy was a big shot first. He didn't work for a damn thing and he still wasn't working. From what I could tell, being the "face" of the company meant jetting around the world flanked by models or standing on yachts flanked by models. *Maybe I'll get to travel,* I thought. *That would be cool at least.*

I woke up the next morning to a torrential downpour. I've been in rainstorms before, of course, but there is something really awful about rainstorms in New York City. For one, the gutters and sewers can never seem to handle the intake. The water backs up and floods the streets and sidewalks and it literally pours down the stairs to the subway stations. Plus, it's almost as if the rain comes down sideways so there is no umbrella that can keep you dry. If you need to get somewhere and you want to stay dry, you're pretty much fucked.

"Great," I said. My hair barely did what I wanted on dry, sunny days, but there was no way it was going to cooperate that day. I tried. I really did. But, of course, by the time I got to my desk, I was soaked to my knees and my hair was frizzing around my face. The message light on my phone was blinking. I checked the message.

"It's Carla. You're on for ten a.m. Good luck! Call me when you're done so we can discuss."

"Seriously?" I grumbled.

I had a couple of hours to dry out and hope the rain let up. It didn't.

I poked my head in Philip's office. "I'm heading out for a bit, Philip," I said.

He looked up from the catalog he was thumbing through. It was a boat catalog. Of course it was. Ugh. "Where you going?" he asked.

"Job interview at XYZ Media," I said.

"Oh, that's impressive," he said, nodding. He looked me up and down, taking in everything from my wild hair to my rumpled skirt to my soggy pantyhose. I looked awful, I knew, but I couldn't fix anything.

"You should call a car," he said, as if I had an extra hundred bucks lying around.

"Yeah, right," I said.

"I'll call you one," he offered.

"Wow, thanks," I said.

"Believe it or not, Jen, I'm not a selfish monster. I am rooting for your success. And it doesn't matter how you look. You have Carleton Corporation on your resume and me as your reference. XYZ would be crazy to turn you down."

"Thank you, Philip," I said.

A few minutes later, the sleek black sedan pulled up to the curb in front of XYZ Media. The rain had let up a bit and I could run to the door. "Will you wait here for me?" I asked the driver.

He shook his head. "No, sorry. I'm only supposed to take you. Man said you gotta get yourself back."

I rolled my eyes. Of course he did, because I only needed to look presentable now, not later. "Right," I said. "Makes total sense."

I walked into the lobby and was immediately assaulted with noise and light coming from giant flat-screen televisions positioned around the room. Carleton was a very staid and somber office environment. XYZ was in your face and loud. I wasn't sure which one I preferred. I noticed that everyone was dressed fairly casually and there was a young, hip vibe. I liked that, but I immediately felt dowdy in my navy pinstripe suit. I clutched my Coach briefcase closer and signed in with the guard.

"Take the express elevator to the fiftieth floor," the guard said.

*Yes!* I thought. *No basement this time.*

I rode the elevator to the fiftieth floor ,where Paula, the human resources director, was waiting to greet me when the doors slid open. "Jen?" she asked.

"Yes, hello," I said. I stuck out my hand and Paula shook it.

"You're wet," she exclaimed.

"Yes, it's raining out there," I said.

"Yes, we have windows, I can see that," Paula replied, wiping her hand on her pant leg.

Carla was right—Paula was indeed a real pain in the ass. "It's just hard to stay dry on a day like this. Sorry about that."

"Uh-huh, let's go through." Paula led me into an enormous conference room. One wall was windows and the other wall was flat-screen TVs. They were turned on to showcase XYZ Media, but they were thankfully muted. I sat across from Paula and I could feel her appraising me. I could tell she did not think I was worth the hype. Carla was a terrific cheerleader, and on most days I could live up to her build-up, but that day I was a frizzy, crumpled, tired mess. It was my first interview again after being out of the game for a while and I was not in the zone. At all.

"What do you consider your greatest strength?" Paula asked.

"I'm a people-pleaser," I lied.

Paula nodded, approvingly. "Is that right?"

"I'm not happy until everyone is happy," I said.

"And your greatest weakness?"

"Well, I think it's related to my strength. I work too hard because I care too much. It's so hard for me to just let work go. Even right now, I'm thinking of a hundred things I need to do back at Carleton before I leave for the day."

"Yes, why are you leaving Carleton?" Paula asked.

*Why am I leaving Carleton?* I thought. *Because my job was eliminated and all the partners are walking around like they won the fucking lottery. They're all getting golden and platinum parachutes and they're buying fucking boats and vacation houses and I'm getting two weeks of severance!* I couldn't tell the truth yet, so I said, "Carleton is a great company and I love being there. It's steady but it's unimaginative. I'm looking for something a bit more exciting. XYZ is doing really incredible things right now in the media world and I'd like to be a part of that."

Paula chortled. "'Unimaginative.' How true. Carleton is damn dinosaur. They haven't done anything earth-shattering in decades."

I smiled, neither agreeing nor disagreeing.

"How are you at working under pressure?"

"Oh, I thrive under pressure. I do some of my best work under pressure," I answered truthfully, because I was under a ton of pressure keeping the company's secret from all of my coworkers.

After I'd convinced Paula that I was smart enough to answer her basic questions, she invited Dex—short for Dexter, of course, the Chairman—to join us.

I knew he was young, but man, I was not prepared! The guy who walked in the door looked like a college student. He looked like a pizza delivery boy. He was young-young. So young. He bounded into the room like he owned the place. Well, I guess that's because he actually did. I didn't know what to do with someone who was practically my peer. I was used to working for men older than my dad. I was stymied. I wasn't sure if I should be formal or casual. From what I'd seen, XYZ Media was casual and laid-back, but this guy was the Chairman—which implied a level of professionalism was required, but I wasn't sure how much. So I didn't say anything. I shook his hand silently and sat back down.

He sat beside Paula and she handed him a clipboard. "Jen seems like a very strong candidate," she said, ignoring the fact that I was a steaming wrinkled mess sitting across the table from them. "She comes highly recommended from the placement agency and Carleton Corporation where she's working now."

"Why are you leaving, Jen?" Dex asked, his blue eyes piercing my soul.

"I-I-I, um, well, you see," I mumbled.

"Carleton is unimaginative," Paula said. "Jen is looking for some excitement in her life."

He nodded. "Of course. Well, you've come to the right place. XYZ invented excitement. Right, Paula?"

"Definitely," Paula said, nodding emphatically.

"What do you like to do in your free time?" Dex asked.

"I have a boyfriend," I blurted a little too loudly and forcefully.

He nodded slowly. "Okay, so you like to spend time with him, then?"

"Yeah. We spend lots of time together. He's great. Really great." I nodded. "So great." I couldn't stop saying great. Dex's blue eyes were making me behave erratically. I loved Ebeneezer. I did. But there was something about Dex that was causing my body parts to stir, if you know what I mean.

Paula saved me again. "I think Dex is trying to find out if you have any hobbies, Jen. Besides hanging out with your boyfriend."

"Oh! Um, yeah. I like to write."

"You're a writer?" he asked, smiling.

Duh! Why hadn't I mentioned that yet? After all, XYZ was a media company! "Yeah, I love to write."

"What have you written?" Dex asked.

"You mean, what have I written or what have I finished?"

"There's a difference?" Paula asked.

I laughed. "Oh yeah, there's a big difference. I start all kinds of stuff. I have tons and tons of first chapters or summaries or just random ideas, but I've never actually finished anything. Because, y'know, that's the hard part."

Both of their faces fell. Fuuuuuuck! I should not have said that. Not finishing is bad. Very, very bad! Admitting that I don't finish what I start wiped out all of my good stuff.

"Hmm," Paula said, making a mark on her clipboard.

Dex furrowed his brow. "I don't know if you're right. Finishing isn't the hardest part. I think starting is the hardest part. If you've started, then you're on your way. You can always go back and finish. You should try finishing one of those ideas, Jen." He hit me with a megawatt smile and babies practically fell out of my vagina.

"Uh-huh," I said, clenching my knees together. I smiled. I liked his thinking! We chitchatted for a few more minutes about writing and I was doing beautifully. The interview was going swimmingly. Dex really liked me. I mean, like a boss would like his employee. He didn't *like* like me. And Paula didn't hate me anymore. I could tell that he thought I would be perfect for the job.

"Okay, Jen," Dex said, suddenly changing the subject. "I have just one more question. This is a question that we're asking all the candidates. It's Paula's idea. It's kind of silly, really. I don't know why Paula's making me ask this. Some sort of way to profile people or something."

"It's just an interesting exercise," Paula said. "There's no wrong answer."

"Sure. No problem. I'm happy to answer it," I said, eager to please and get started at my new, fancy job with my hot boss.

"Okay. If you were an animal what animal would you be, and why?"

"If I was an animal?" I asked, confused. "Do you mean, do I like animals?"

Paula spoke up. "No. We want to know what animal you think best describes your personality and why."

Was she fucking kidding me? What kind of question was that? I had aced all of her general HR questions. What was this nonsense? I was not prepared for a random animal question.

I realized I was taking too long to answer and I could tell I was losing my shine. Dex's interest was waning and I had to say something quickly. I decided not to overthink it, just go with whatever popped into my mind. So I blurted out the first thing that came to me: "I'm a koala bear."

Paula nodded and made a mark on her clipboard. "Interesting. Go on," she said. "Why are you a koala bear?"

Aha! She liked it! I had chosen correctly! There was no stopping me now!

"Well, I'm a koala bear, because I look little and fuzzy and sometimes a little sleepy, even. But if you get too close and irritate me, I can get feisty and I have pretty big claws that will get you." And then I stood up and growled. "Rawrrrrr."

Paula and Dex both jumped a little. Paula scribbled something on her paper that looked like a giant X and Dex went completely dead in the eyes.

I'd lost him! He clearly thought I was crazy. I wasn't crazy! I had to get Dex back on my side. I had to make him see that I was the right person to marry—I mean hire. The question was stupid! Didn't he see when you ask a stupid question, you get a stupid answer? I scrambled to salvage the interview, so I added, "Oh! And koalas are cute—just like me. You think I'm cute, right, Dex? Or at least I think you did just a few minutes ago."

Dex shifted uncomfortably in his seat.

And then, just in case I wasn't sure I'd completely lost the job yet, I sealed the deal by WINKING at the man.

An hour later I was back at my desk and on the phone with Carla. "Did you hit on the Chairman of XYZ?" she asked.

"No comment," I replied. "What else you got?"

Carla sighed. "I don't know. I guess I can see if the Bronx Zoo has an opening for a randy koala bear."

"I'm a very hardworking, randy koala bear, Carla," I said. "Get it right, please."

# CHAPTER 10

## I WAS WRONG BEFORE—I DON'T GET PAID ENOUGH FOR THIS SHIT

IT TOOK A LOT MORE INTERVIEWS, but I finally landed a job a few months before my job with Philip would officially end. When I told him I'd found a new position and would be leaving in two weeks he was actually kind of pissed off.

"Really, Jen? Now? Can't you delay your start day about sixty days or so?"

"Why would I do that, Philip?" I asked.

"To show your loyalty to the company."

"Loyalty?" I snorted. I couldn't believe his audacity. "Loyalty? Yes, because the company has shown me so much loyalty these last few months."

"You are part of the Carleton family, Jen. Isn't that worth something?"

"I don't know, Philip. Is it? Because it doesn't seem like Carleton cares much for the family these days."

"You're being incredibly selfish, Jen," Philip said. "If nothing else, think of the transition team. You're abandoning us when we need you most. You've never been more important to the company than you are right now."

I shook my head at his logic. "I'm sure the transition will go smoothly with or without me," I said.

"You've just doubled all of our workloads because you won't be a team player and stay until the end. Tanya is staying."

"Philip, I can't stay until the end. I don't have the golden parachutes the rest of you have. You're going to retire to the South of France in sixty days. Tanya got a completely different deal than me, which doesn't seem fair, but that's a whole other complaint. You offered me two weeks. I can't be that important if I'm only worth two weeks. I'm sorry, Philip, but there's no way I'm staying to the end. My contract says I must give two weeks notice, so consider yourself notified. I can call Carla and get you a temp by tomorrow and she can shadow me until I'm gone, but that's the best I can do."

"Well, I must say I'm very disappointed in you, Jen. I really expected better from you. This is not the Midwestern work ethic I hired you for."

"I guess I've been in New York too long, Philip," I said. "And the cynicism has worn off on me."

Philip wouldn't let me call Carla and get him a temp. Instead he and Tanya made a huge production of taking all the burden on themselves. Tanya even offered to cancel a cruise she'd booked a year before. "I really don't mind canceling," she said. "I'll have plenty of time off soon enough."

"What do you think she should do, Jen?" Philip asked me.

I think he was trying to make me feel guilty, but I really didn't give a shit. I was so ready to get out of the toxic environment that was Carleton Corporation, and if Philip and Tanya wanted to be martyrs, let them!

I was pissed off at the way everything had been handled. I was furious with the partners who were literally skipping around the office while the worker bees trudged through the transition knowing that their days were numbered. Everyone was having their jobs eliminated, but the partners all had huge buyouts and the rest of us got pink slips. Over lunch, the office drones would compare resumes and swap interview nightmare stories while the executives thumbed through real estate pamphlets and high-fived one another.

Every day I opened mail for the Chairman from Carleton Corporation's factory workers in Middle America. Their stories were painful to read. Many of them had worked for the Chairman and his company for several generations and were devastated to learn that they too would soon be out of work. They talked about entire towns that would be wiped out, because their local economies depended upon Carleton. They begged the Chairman to reconsider, or even just to visit and explain to them in person why he was selling a company that they and their fathers and their fathers' fathers had worked for. Why was he intent on destroying their livelihood? they asked. Every morning I read and cataloged the letters and then passed them on to Cynthia, the Chairman's assistant. I have no idea what happened to them after that. They probably went directly into the "circular file," as they liked to say (i.e., the trashcan), without so much as a glance, let alone a reply.

The phrase "It's just business" rang hollow when I thought of those letters. Each one of them was written by a human being who trusted the company, who believed the company would do the right thing by them. With the swish of a pen, those jobs were eliminated, traded in to line the pockets of already wealthy men with even more money.

Some of these men had so much they couldn't spend it all in a lifetime. It was nauseating to be around that office, so I was thrilled when Carla called me up to say, "Mr. Ogden loved you. You're in, kid."

"That's great news," I said, relieved.

"Yeah, you're really moving up in the world, Jen," Carla said. "Booker and Associates is big time."

"Yeah, I think it's going to be great."

"Ogden's the real deal. You'll finally get to do some real writing."

"I know. I'm excited," I said.

I wasn't surprised when Carla called. I could tell that Mr. Ogden had liked me. Believe it or not, once again my Midwestern roots had gotten me the job. And for once, so did my big mouth.

My first interview at Booker was conducted by the head of human resources, Rita. I went in completely blind. Not that Carla ever gave me a lot of information, but this time she could only give me vague details. She said Booker was a private consulting firm and I'd be working for one of the top partners. He needed someone who could write his speeches and manage all of his board seats.

"He's super important and powerful, or whatever," Carla said. "Rita's kind of being stupid about it, so just play dumb.

Meanwhile, I had totally done an extensive internet search the night before but Carla told me to pretend I knew nothing, because Rita was insistent that I couldn't even know the guy's name until I passed the background check.

Rita sat me down and asked what I knew about the job. "Not much," I said.

Rita nodded. "That's good," she said. "Around here we really value our executives's privacy." When she pronounced the word "privacy" the way Philip would I knew she took herself way too seriously. No normal person says "prih-vicy" on purpose. We went through all the usual questions about strengths and weaknesses and why I was leaving my current position and blah, blah, blah. I could tell the truth this time and I managed not to wink or roar at her and kept my composure long enough to get through the first round.

Then she brought me back for a second round with a group. There were three of us this time and I could tell that I had more experience than the other two combined, so I got overconfident and kind of bossy. No, not kind of bossy. Really bossy. At one point I said something like, "Just get me in front of Mr. Ogden and this will be a done deal."

Rita did not like that. "Mr. Ogden is incredibly busy. He does not have time to interview candidates," she said, all snippy.

"Well he has to meet me at some point, doesn't he?" I said.

"He'll meet you on your first day," Rita replied. "*If* I decide to hire you."

"If? Oh come on, Rita. We both know I'm the best candidate," I said.

I could hear Carla screaming in my head. *Stop, you dumb cocky broad! Rita is not someone you mess with!*

I must not have pissed off Rita too much, though, because a few days later I was back again for my third interview. This time I would finally be meeting with the rest of Mr. Ogden's staff to see what they thought of me. We were in his private conference room when he burst through the door. He was an older man with messy hair and his suit coat was tucked into the back of his trousers. *This guy is powerful and important?*

His lead assistant, Ambrose, jumped up to intervene. "We're just finishing up in here, Mr. Ogden. I didn't think you'd be back so soon!"

Mr. Ogden waved him off. "What's going on in here, Ambrose?" he asked.

"Let's get you back to your office, Mr. Ogden," his driver, Carlos, offered.

"Are you interviewing? Without me?" Mr. Ogden demanded.

"We didn't want to bother you, sir," said Ambrose.

"Bother me?" Mr. Ogden said. "Shouldn't I be the one to decide who I hire?"

Ambrose stammered, "W-w-well, you never met me before I was hired."

"Nor me, sir," Carlos said.

"Well, maybe I should have!" Mr. Ogden said, his eyes blazing.

Ambrose and Carlos looked shocked. I don't know why, but something about the way Mr. Ogden said that phrase made me realize he was teasing them and they weren't getting it, but I did. So I laughed.

His sharp eyes turned on me. "You think that's funny?"

I smiled. "Yeah, I do."

Mr. Ogden wagged his bushy eyebrows at me. "Give me that," he said, taking my resume from his second assistant, Mary Anne. He glanced at it. "Kansas, huh?" His sharp eyes were on me again.

I squirmed a bit. "Yes," I said.

"I'm a Midwesterner too," he said. "I left when I was

twelve and never went back. Kind of a hell hole. But I'm from the Midwest. Did Rita tell you that?"

"No, actually, she didn't tell me anything about you," I replied.

"You're kidding? You don't know who I am?"

"Not really," I said. I knew it was a mistake to tell rich, powerful men that you have no clue who they are, but I didn't want Rita to catch me in a lie down the road. Besides, I could see it irritated Mr. Ogden that Rita hadn't filled me in. *Good,* I thought. *She's annoying.*

"Carlos, bring around the car. I'm going to see Brooke Astor." He looked at me. "You know who she is, right?"

"I think she's kind of important," I said. "I know there was an Astor on the *Titanic*. I assume they're related. I don't really keep up with the society page."

The phones in the office started ringing and Mr. Ogden said to Ambrose and Mary Anne, "Those phones aren't going to answer themselves."

Ambrose looked torn. I could tell he did not want to leave me alone with Mr. Ogden. There was a hierarchy and I was violating it. But he couldn't bear to not do his job either. "Mary Anne can handle the phones," Ambrose said, sitting down beside Mr. Ogden.

Mr. Ogden ignored him. Mary Anne stuck her head back in the door. "Mr. Ogden, that one anchor you like... from that one morning show...is on the line."

"Who?" Mr. Ogden snapped.

"The one...you and your wife had dinner with her last week..." I didn't know why Mary Anne was being so coy. It was weird.

"Katie or Diane?" I wanted to ask.

"I'll call her back," he said.

Ambrose practically squeaked. "Are you sure, Mr. Ogden? It might be important. I can handle this."

Mr. Ogden continued to ignore Ambrose. "I'm a Midwesterner and I like Midwesterners," Mr. Ogden said. "Simple people with simple needs."

I thought that was code for, *She'll work cheap*, so I said, "I'm not that simple. You should see my AmEx bill."

He chuckled. "A simple girl with expensive tastes, then."

Mary Anne stuck her head back in the room again. "Ambrose," she whispered. "I need you. The phones are going crazy."

Ambrose glared at Mary Anne, but got up and followed her out. He gave me a look over his shoulder that said, *I'm watching you*.

"Are you married?" Mr. Ogden asked me.

"Legally, I don't think you can ask me that," I said, raising an eyebrow.

He laughed a great big booming laugh. "I'm just curious about who you are." I later found out that he rarely hired married women. Married women didn't work late enough. Married women wanted children and Mr. Ogden did not like his staff to have children. Children were needy.

"Next question," I said.

We chatted for another twenty minutes, which I realized years later was an eternity to Mr. Ogden. He parceled his life into ten-minute chunks and very few people got twenty uninterrupted minutes with him. We had an easy rapport. He was a smart aleck and I called him on his bullshit.

As he headed out for his meeting with Brooke Astor I heard him call over his shoulder, "Make her the offer, Rita."

That was the real reason I wasn't surprised when Carla called.

There would be a couple of instances over the years where I'd overstep and just about get fired, but for the most part Mr. Ogden and I got along great.

One of the times I almost got fired was when I arrived at the office to find a brown paper lunch sack on my desk. "What's this?" I asked Ambrose.

Carlos giggled and became very interested in the sole of his shoe.

Ambrose looked up from his work. "It's for you. I've decided you're in charge of that area of the office now," he said.

"What is it?"

I started to open the sack to peer inside and Carlos yelled, "No! Don't! It's not for lady's eyes." English wasn't Carlos's first language and sometimes things he said got lost in the translation. I figured this was one of those times.

"What are you talking about?" I reached into the bag and pulled out a glass jelly jar with the label ripped off. A piece of masking tape was on the lid that read, "Sample." Inside was what I can only describe as a pile of shit. An actual, literal, pile of solid human waste. "What the fuck?"

"I told you, not for lady's eyes," Carlos said.

"Calm down, Jen, Mr. Ogden will hear you," Ambrose said in a panicky voice. Ambrose spent half his day living in fear of Mr. Ambrose hearing me raise my voice.

"What the fuck is this?" I asked. "Is it what I think it is?"

Ambrose nodded. "As you know, Mr. Ogden likes to

make sure that everyone he knows is always on top of his or her health," he said.

That was an understatement. Mr. Ogden had doctors' appointments just about every day. As far as I could tell, everything he did or took was preventative, but then he'd argue all of his medical intervention was how he stayed so healthy.

"Every once in a while a stool sample is sent in for testing. This needs to be delivered to this address in the next hour." Ambrose handed me a piece of paper.

"This is his shit?" I asked, horrified.

Ambrose shrugged. "I have no idea who gave the sample, I only know Mr. Ogden wants it delivered."

"Can't we call a courier?" I asked.

Ambrose shook his head. "No, Mr. Ogden wants someone on his staff to deliver it. No one else."

"Well, I don't think this is my job. I write his reports."

"We all pitch in around here," Ambrose said.

"What about Carlos? Why can't he take it?"

Ambrose shook his head. "No, Carlos has to be here at all times in case Mr. Ogden wants to leave the building."

"He has nothing on his calendar until this afternoon," I argued. "Carlos could go real fast."

"I can't," Carlos said. "Mr. Ogden's appointments change all the time. He will be mad if I'm gone. I never take the poop. Ever."

"So you've done this before? Who did this before I got here?" I asked.

"Mary Anne and I took turns," said Ambrose. "But she's too busy now with her new responsibilities."

"Okay, so let's take turns. You go first since I'm new and I might get lost," I said.

"It doesn't work that way anymore, Jen," Ambrose said.

"You and I have very different roles in this office. And we need to keep those roles separated. For instance, I always answer phones and schedule Mr. Ogden's appointments and you...you do whatever it is that you do."

"I don't deliver shit across town," I said. "This was not in my job description." *What the fuck is wrong with these rich dudes?* I wondered. *I thought picking up Mike's dirty drawers was bad, but this is worse.*

I grabbed the jar and marched into Mr. Ogden's office. Now, let me tell you: this was just not done. You didn't just walk into his office and interrupt him. You let Ambrose determine if now was a good time and then you would have him announce you and then you'd scoot in real fast and get what you needed from Mr. Ogden and scoot out real quick. I didn't do that. I just rolled in and plopped the poop on his mahogany desk.

"What is this?" Mr. Ogden said, frowning, as if he didn't recognize the jar he'd perhaps shat into that morning.

"It's a sample," I said. "Ambrose thinks it's my job to haul this thing across town."

"Okay, well, if that's what Ambrose thinks," he said, shrugging. "Ambrose knows what needs to be done."

"I'm not going to do that," I said. "There have got to be medical couriers or something. People who are trained to deal with samples and such like this."

Mr. Ogden glared at me. "Do you like working here, Jen?" he asked.

"Yes, of course," I said.

"So then why are we arguing about this? Your job is unique. Your job is rewarding. But sometimes not every part of it is as rewarding as other parts. There are many different facets to your job and this is one of them."

"I wasn't told about this when I was hired," I said.

"Would you have passed on the job if you had been?" "I would have told whoever crapped in that jar that you should give samples in a doctor's office. They know how to handle that stuff."

"So you're too good to do your job?"

I didn't say anything. I wanted to say, *I'm too good to do this part of my job. This isn't even sanitary. Plus, I don't think this sample can be evaluated properly. It's in a mother-fucking jelly jar!"*

Before I could say anything Ambrose stuck his head in. "Mr. Ogden, line one for you."

Mr. Ogden and I stared one another down and then finally he picked up the phone. I left the room, leaving the sample on his desk. A few minutes later Mr. Ogden buzzed for Ambrose. He emerged from his office with the jar. "He said, 'Tell her to take it or she's fired!'" Ambrose said, putting the jar on my desk. I was furious. I stormed out of the office. "Where are you going?" Ambrose asked, like he was my fucking timekeeper.

"To the restroom. I need to wash my hands after touching that thing!" I said.

I stayed in the bathroom for a few minutes debating what I was going to do. Was I really going to draw the line in the sand and say, *This is it. I will not cross this line?* It was a good job and it was interesting and exciting and I was writing a lot and learning a lot. Would I give all of that up because I was too proud to touch a jar full of someone's poo?

I came back to the office, deflated. I didn't want to lose my job, so I was prepared to take the shit to the doctor's office. I got back to my desk and found the sample gone. "Where did it go?" I asked Ambrose.

He scowled at me. "Carlos was afraid you were going to

get fired so he took it for you and now he'll probably get fired if Mr. Ogden goes looking for him. But the next time is your turn. No arguing," he said.

But there wasn't a next time. I don't know if Mr. Ogden realized that it was humiliating and degrading to have someone's warm dump on your desk or if the doctor said, "Dude! That sample was so contaminated with Smucker's we couldn't tell anything. Next time, it needs to be done in the office. Get the business done here in a clean, sterile environment." Either way, Mr. Ogden never brought another sample to the office.

When Carlos returned I thanked him.

"I told you," he said. "Not for lady's eyes." He shuddered. "Not for my eyes either."

THE REAL ESTATE YEARS

## CHAPTER 11

### TOWELS ARE FOR CLOSERS

IN 2001 I threw down the gauntlet and told Ebeneezer it was time to put up or shut up. We'd dated for several years. I'd dumped him twice and both times he came back, and so I dumped him a third and final time. I was closing in on thirty, I was working at a job where I was expected to be on call twelve hours a day. I had gone as high as I could go and unless I wanted to be an overworked assistant for the rest of my life, I needed to get out. I wanted kids, and Mr. Ogden had made it very clear that mothers had no place in his office. Plus, I didn't want to get home only in time to kiss my kids goodnight. Something had to change.

"We need to get married and move away or we need to break up," I told Ebeneezer.

Even though I'd been contemplating this idea for months, it was the first Ebeneezer heard of it and he was more than a little surprised. "Then I guess we break up," he said.

"Fine," I said, showing him to the door.

But he couldn't quit me, and within a day he was back and down on one knee.

I knew it wasn't feasible for us to get married and raise kids in New York City. I couldn't imagine three or four of us squeezed into my tiny Queens apartment, but we couldn't afford a bigger place. Neither of us had flexibility with our job, and so our kids would be in daycare and I had no idea how we'd afford that either. And the thought of private school tuition down the road gave me a panic attack. We had to move. It was the only solution.

"I'll marry you," I said. "But we need to move back to Kansas."

"Kansas?" Ebeneezer said. "I was thinking Long Island was far enough."

"I've been doing a lot of thinking," I said. "Kansas is where we should be."

"But you hated it when you lived there," he said.

"I know. It sucks for single people, but it's good for families. The public schools are good. It's affordable. We can buy a house for what I pay in rent here. A whole house!"

"With a garage?"

"Two garages," I said.

"That does sound nice," he said.

"My parents could help take care of a baby," I said.

"A baby!" Ebeneezer exclaimed. "We just got engaged. Slow down."

"I can't slow down, Ebeneezer, my uterus is dusty."

"What about jobs?" Ebeneezer asked. "What will we do for money?"

"You could get a transfer with your company." Ebeneezer was a sales representative for a huge pharmaceutical company in those days. "They need drug dealers all over the country."

He nodded. "That's true. I could put in a request to

move. What will you do though? Mr. Ogden won't let you work remotely."

"No, he'd never do that," I said. "I'm going to sell real estate."

"What?"

A few months before, I'd been home for Easter and my uncle Reuben asked me how things were going in New York. It was probably a rhetorical question, but I unloaded on the poor man. I let him know that Ebeneezer was dragging his feet to get married and I wasn't getting any younger. I wanted a family but I also wanted a career. I told him that I was unhappy in New York. I was always tired and grimy. I didn't have enough money to enjoy the city and I was sick of people. I wanted to move away from New York, but I wasn't sure what I'd do for a job in Kansas. I didn't want to go back to the engineering firm (and really, I couldn't, because I hadn't left on good terms, plus Uncle Monty had taken his gold watch and retired so my hookup was gone) but working for Mr. Ogden was draining the life out of me. My life was not my own anymore. I had to find something new.

"Have you thought about real estate?" Uncle Reuben asked.

"Sales?" I wrinkled my nose. Uncle Reuben worked in real estate, so of course he thought it was a good idea. I was way too shy to be in sales. "No, that's Ebeneezer's area. I suck at sales."

"Real estate isn't your typical sales job," Reuben assured me. "It's more of a relationship business. I think you could be good at it, Jen. You need a network of people to rely on at the beginning and you have a big network here in Kansas City. It would make sense for you to do it here. It's fairly inexpensive to start out. I think you could be successful at it."

The more Uncle Reuben talked, the more I warmed up to the idea. I could set my own hours and work from home or the office. I'd be an independent contractor, so I'd be my own boss. Ultimately I'd answer to a broker, but he wouldn't be breathing down my neck or scheduling pointless meetings with me. I could pick and choose my clients. The best part was no more annoying coworkers and office politics to deal with.

"And I've seen lots of women with children who made a career in real estate. You could have it all—a career and kids. Aren't you ready for a career, Jen?"

Uncle Reuben sold me. "Yes!" I said.

———

Ebeneezer and I moved to Kansas, and a month after our wedding I started real estate school. Reuben was right. The sales part was easy, because I didn't waste time on people who didn't need me. I wasn't selling lipstick. Every woman can use a new tube of lipstick and so makeup consultants don't give up on their first no. But not everyone needs a new house. If they say no, I move on. But if they do need a new house, then they stop and listen to what I'm saying. I enjoyed the classes and I learned quickly how to overcome objections and help guide my clients to the best purchase they could afford. I could see a career in real estate. Finally, I was on my way!

I was really lucky because I landed my first client the day after I got my license. Emaline was a friend and she was looking to buy her first house. On our first day working together, I loaded up my fancy leather Coach outlet briefcase with information sheets about every house we'd be looking at and a blank contract (because I was taught to always be prepared to close the deal). I took my car to the car wash because my broker had told me that it was my calling card and I would be judged by it. He also told me that my car sucked and no amount of washing would help it and so as soon as I had some money, I needed to buy a new car.

"If you show up in a crappy car, people will think you're a crappy Realtor, Jen. Buy an expensive car. Fake it until you make it," he said.

Emaline knew she was my first client and so I didn't need to fake it with her, but I vowed to have a new car within six months. And in order to do that, I needed to sell a house to Emaline (and about thirty other people).

Emaline and I drove to the first house on the list. I was nervous and excited. I was going to help my friend make the biggest investment of her young life! She was trusting me with her future! I didn't want to do anything wrong. I checked and double-checked that the temperature in the car was perfect for Emaline ("It was fine when you asked thirty seconds ago, Jen, and it's still fine."). I offered to buy her a coffee to enjoy while we toured homes (the Starbucks kind, not the cheap QuikTrip kind). I pointed out all of the interesting and unique features of the neighborhood we were driving through ("I don't have kids, Jen, I don't care if there's an elementary school within walking distance.").

We arrived at a nice split-entry home with a tidy lawn and a flag flying from a pole in the front yard. It was three bedrooms, two full baths, and an eat-in kitchen, with a finished lower level. All of the things Emaline had asked for.

"Here we are!" I said. "Your new home!"

"Stop that, Jen. Are you going to do that every time?" Emaline said. "Be normal, please."

"Sorry, it's just that my broker told me I should introduce every house this way so that my client could really see him or herself living there. It puts you in the right mind-set for home ownership."

"Well my mind-set is you're annoying me. We can't do that all day," Emaline said. "I picked you because I don't trust Realtors, but I trust you. But I'll find another Realtor if you get all smarmy on me."

"Message received," I said. "No more smarmy Realtor stuff."

"All right, let's see this one." Emaline sighed.

"You don't sound excited," I said. "You should be excited. It meets all of your criteria."

"It's not anywhere close to where I want to live, Jen," Emaline said.

"But you can't afford where you want to live," I reminded her.

"I know, so it's going to take some getting used to."

"This one is great!" I said. "New paint, new carpet..."

"Uh-huh."

We climbed up the stairs to the front door and I was too busy selling the joint to remember the most important piece of advice my broker gave me before I headed out that morning.

I used my master key and I got the front door unlocked and we walked in. The house was staged beautifully. The rooms looked bright and spacious. The new paint was a perfect neutral beige color that coordinated nicely with the new beige carpet. We made our way into the beige kitchen and were immediately impressed with the size of the room. "Nice counters," I said.

"They are," Emaline agreed. "The cabinets are ugly though."

"Easy fix," I assured her, even though I had never

painted cabinets in my life. Those home remodeling shows made it look easy.

We found the beige rec room in the basement, and Emaline had to admit that it was better than she'd anticipated. "This is kind of cozy," she said.

"Let's go upstairs," I said. "Wait until you see the master. The online pictures make the master bedroom look terrific."

Emaline followed me up the stairs and I continued to prattle about all the features I could detect, including the sturdiness of the banister. Yeah, I pointed out how sturdy the banister was, like that was a selling point or something. I wanted to sell that house!

There was a hallway at the top of the stairs with four doors, all shut tightly.

"Which one is the master?" Emaline asked.

"I don't know," I said. "Is it door number one?" I selected a door and pushed it open dramatically. It revealed a bedroom that was set up like a home office. The overhead light was on, the computer on the desk was on and the printer was humming in standby mode.

"Does someone work here?" Emaline asked.

"I don't know. Maybe?" I said. "Looks like they left in a hurry. Must have realized they had a showing coming up and wanted to get out of here before we arrived. They should have shut down though. That might be personal stuff on there."

"Yeah," said Emaline. "Strange."

"We won't be nosy," I said, closing the door behind us.

We tried door number two. That was another bedroom. This one was set up like a workout room with a punching bag and free weights. "Single guy?" I speculated.

"Probably," Emaline said. "I can't see a woman living in this place. It's so sparse...and beige."

The third door hid a hall bath with: "Double sinks," I said. "That's a feature."

"Uh-huh," Emaline said, bored out of her mind. "Except I will live here alone. I won't need double sinks."

"Helps with resale," I said.

"Great."

"Well, I think we know where the master is now," I said, reaching for door number four. I turned the knob and yelled, "Ta-da!"

I was facing Emaline when I opened the door, because I wanted to see her reaction. The reaction of my very first client seeing the nicest master bedroom she could afford. This was it! Emaline was on a tight budget and I wanted her to see the nicest house first even though my broker said to make it last so she'd be a little dead inside by the time we got there and then she'd appreciate just how nice this house was and she'd be more likely to buy. I didn't want to do that to Emaline. She was my friend and I wanted the best for her. I wanted her to be thrilled. When she saw that (beige) room I expected her face to light up and maybe she'd even exclaim, "Wow" or something. I expected her to say, "Yes, this is it, Jen! Well done!" Instead her eyes went wide and were they frightened, maybe? I couldn't tell. She did exclaim. But instead of "Wow" she said, "What the—"

And the naked man who had just stepped out of the shower and was standing in the middle of room finished her sentence: "—fuck are you doing here?" I had forgotten the number one rule of real estate:

ALWAYS RING THE DOORBELL AND
ANNOUNCE YOURSELF.

"Oh my God!" I yelled, trying to avert my eyes but also search the room for a towel. "I'm so sorry! The door was—"

"Locked!" the man yelled, covering his twig and berries with his hands.

"Yes, yes, it was," I said. "I used my key. I had an appointment. I called ahead."

The man yelled, "I don't care! Get out!"

Emaline and I scurried out of the room and down the stairs. I hesitated at the front door. My broker said to always leave my business card in a house after I'd shown it so the listing agent could follow up and get some feedback on the listing. *Should I leave a card?* I wondered. I really didn't want anyone to know my name.

"Go, go!" Emaline pushed me toward the door.

"I need to leave a card." I fumbled in my bag.

"Just go! I just saw that man's junk. I am never going to buy this house!"

"But that master..." I said woefully. "It's the best one you can afford."

Emaline bought a house a few weeks later, but it wasn't as nice as the naked man's house.

# CHAPTER 12

## THE TOUGHEST JOB I'LL
## EVER LOVE

WHEN I WAS thirty-six weeks pregnant with my first child, Gomer, I went into labor. Ironically, I went into labor on my last real working day. Being a self-employed Realtor, I got to pick and choose the days I would work. But being a self-employed Realtor, I also didn't get any paid time off, so my schedule was flexible and I could take as much time as I needed as long as I didn't want any money.

My pregnancy up until that point had been uneventful. I mean, after I figured out I didn't have a tumor and instead my birth control had failed and I was twelve weeks pregnant. Other than that, everything was terrific and I didn't have any complications except extreme exhaustion. However, I wanted a few weeks to get his room finished and get myself ready for my new job: mother. I was Superwoman in those days and I planned everything. I'd scheduled three closings for that day and I figured once I was done, I'd take the remaining four weeks or so off to nest and sleep—but mostly sleep.

My new boss, Gomer, was quite demanding and he decided we needed to meet sooner. So I found myself in a hospital bed hooked up to monitors and drips, surrounded by my files, trying to get everything sorted before he made his arrival. I made some calls and managed to find a colleague willing to take over my last few closings. I was quite proud of myself that I got everything covered, and by nine that night, two of my clients were closed, the third was postponed for later in the week (because my client was insisting that I be there for his closing, and silly me, thinking I'd be up and at 'em by Friday, I'd said, "No problem"), and I'd pushed out a tiny baby.

After getting Gomer cleaned up we took all of the mandatory first child pictures and then finally it was time to rest. The nurses convinced me that I'd worked hard and I needed a break, so I should send Gomer to the nursery for the night.

The Hubs and I looked at each other. He was scowling at the cot beside my bed and already thinking about our bed at home waiting for him. He had no desire to sleep on that roll-away and he had to think of a plan, but he knew he would have to make it my idea or else it would never work.

"You know I'll do whatever you want, Jen. I'm happy to sleep on that little bed. I just think *you* could use a break. We could send Gomer to the nursery and then I could just go home and get out of your hair so you could get a peaceful rest without me bothering you. You've worked so hard...you must be exhausted. You look like you could use a good sleep," the Hubs offered.

I hesitated. I was brand-new to this motherhood job and I didn't know what to do. There wasn't a job description I could follow. Did good mothers send their newborns to the nursery on their first night? My sleepy brain said, "Yeeessss. Dooooo it." So I let the Hubs go home and Gomer go to the nursery and I drifted off to sleep.

Within a few hours a burly nurse was banging down my door and flipping on my overhead light. "Wake up, Mom," she said. "There's a problem with your baby."

I sat up in bed and tried to comprehend what she was saying. Mom? Was that me? Problem? "What's going on?" I asked.

"Gomer's having some trouble."

I looked around and realized he was not with her. "Where is he?"

"They'll bring him by in a minute for you to see him. You need to know that the nursery was full last night and so we had to keep him at the nurses' station," she said.

"My baby slept at the nurses' station?" I asked, horrified.

"You know what? It was a good thing he was there, because someone noticed his body temp was dropping."

"That's because he was sleeping in a hallway!" I argued. I felt like shit. I had one job and I was failing. How could I have sent my baby away? If I'd kept him in my room I would have kept him warm. When he left he only had on a t-shirt and a thin blanket. I had a ton of baby blankets friends had knitted me. I should have wrapped him in one! It was fucking November—*of course* he was cold! "I sent my baby to sleep in the hall, all because I wanted an uninterrupted night of sleep! What's wrong with me?" I couldn't hold back the tears.

"Calm down. That had nothing to do with it," the nurse said. "Anyway, the temp isn't his biggest problem though," she said. "Twenty minutes ago he gagged and coughed up a lot of mucus and blood. He stopped breathing and we had to clear his airway."

"Oh my God!"

"Yeah, but because his temp had dropped, we were keeping a close eye on him so we caught it right away.

He's fine now. It's a good thing we had him with us," she said.

I wiped my tears and patted myself on the back and thought, *See? I was a good mother to send him to the nursery!*

She continued, "We cleared his airway. I don't think for a second you could have done that."

*Fuuuck. She's right. I suck at being a mother.*

"He's breathing on his own and everything, but we have to send him for tests." She stepped out in the hall and wheeled Gomer's Isolette into the room. "You should say goodbye to him."

I burst into tears again. *Where are they taking my baby? What's wrong with him? Why didn't I keep him with me?*

I kissed him and he was gone.

The Hubs arrived a few hours later and finding me in a semi-catatonic state and Gomer gone, he was more than a little upset with me.

"What sort of tests?" he asked repeatedly once I filled him in on Gomer's episode at the nurses' station.

"I don't know!" I yelled after the tenth time he asked me. "She didn't say. She just said he needed tests. She's a nurse. I am not. I figured she knew best and I should not argue with her!"

"Okay, but did you even ask if you could go with him?"

*Oh. Yeah. That. I guess I could have done that. Add another tick in the crappy mom column.* "I wasn't invited!"

"*Invited?* He's your child!"

"She said, 'Say goodbye' and so I did!"

It didn't help that the nurse I'd spoken to had gone home and no one at the nurses' station had a clue where

Gomer had gone and no one really seemed interested in helping us find him.

"He'll be back soon, I'm sure," a nurse said.

After several hours of my child being gone, a doctor came in and told us that he was being admitted to the Neonatal Intensive Care Unit—NICU. He had passed all of his tests, but he was still having a difficult time maintaining his body temperature and now he was too weak to eat.

Okay, let me just stop right here. To a brand-new mother who'd never once considered the possibility that her child might end up in the NICU, this news sounded devastating. Looking back now, I realize that this was not that big of a deal. There were babies in the NICU *literally* fighting for their lives, and my child was relatively healthy in comparison. However, since this was *my* baby, *his* health was what I focused on. It didn't matter that he was the giant five-pound baby in there. He was my giant and he was failing and we needed to do what we could to get him healthy and get him home.

It was the second or third night Gomer was in NICU when I gave birth for a second time.

The Hubs and I had gone down to the nursery to feed Gomer around midnight. I couldn't feed him. My milk still hadn't come in and I was too shaky to hold him. When I mentioned this to the nurse she smiled kindly and said, "Oh, that's normal for mothers with advanced maternal age."

I was thirty-two, I wasn't fifty! No one believed me when I told them I'd felt like shit ever since his delivery. So much so that there were many times I felt too weak to get out of bed to visit Gomer. The NICU nurses were growing suspicious and the Hubs had glimpsed a note in Gomer's file that said "Mother is not bonding with child."

*Fuck you, nurse!* I wasn't given the chance to bond with my child. We were really only welcome to visit the NICU during feeding times. The rest of the time he was to be left alone so he could rest and grow stronger. Meanwhile, I had debilitating back pain and my arms trembled so much I was worried I might drop Gomer every time I held him. Whenever I asked for a chair to sit and hold him I was told there was only one chair and it was for "nursing mothers." (It reminded me of "Coffee is for closers.") I took this personally as a total smack in the face because my milk had not yet come in and my starving baby was being kept alive with a formula concoction that was fed to him through a tube up his nose. The nurses couldn't tell me enough times how much faster Gomer would recover if I'd just be willing to whip out my boob and feed him. I kept saying my milk wasn't in and they looked at me like I was willing it not to come. Instead of believing that there might be something medically wrong with me preventing this lifesaving nectar from reaching Gomer's lips, they just went ahead and blamed it on my lack of will and desire.

So, if I was awake I'd shuffle down to the NICU to say hello to Gomer and watch the Hubs change him and feed him, and the nurses would write down their judgmental comments in the file. I never saw them judging the fifteen-year-old meth-head mom with the baby in the next Isolette. I'm not sure what was wrong with her baby (we weren't allowed to talk about it), but he was very tiny and looked incredibly frail. I'm sure all the meth didn't help.

"Hey, kid. What's up? I have no idea what to say to you," she'd mumble to her baby.

"Good job talking to your baby, Lurleen! He hears your

voice and knows that you're close by. You're such a very good mother! Tomorrow we'll work on some encouraging phrases, but really great job today!" The nurse would practically clap her hands and offer Lurleen a gold star. Then her eyes would go dead and she'd turn on me. "Hello, Jen. Still no desire to hold your baby today?"

"I would love to hold him, but I need a chair. My arms are really weak and I'm afraid I will drop him."

"Bedelia has the chair right now. *She's* breastfeeding. Still no milk?"

Yeah, there was only one chair in the whole place! It was insane. I could not work under those conditions! "Not yet. The lactation consultant was in twice today. She helped me pump half a milliliter of colostrum this morning. I sent it with my husband to feed to Gomer."

The lactation consultant was a whole level of embarrassment I'd never known. It was so cute when I thought it was bad to have to pick up a dirty pair of underwear or deliver a jelly jar of poop. Now I sat topless in a room where the door opened without so much as a knock exposing my knockers to everyone in the hallway. I let complete strangers touch my breasts and help me figure out how to cram my stupid large nipples into the tiny cones on the breast pump. I sent my husband to find me larger cones, nipple shields, and lanolin. I let a woman with the iciest hands manipulate and prod my breasts to stimulate my milk production. I was no longer Jen the Person, I was now a body that was probed and poked, all because my new boss demanded to be fed. My whole job now was to hook myself up to the industrial-size pump and mine for liquid gold.

"Uh-huh. We got it," the nurse said. "Excuse me. I need to make a note in Gomer's file."

The Hubs and I were headed back to my room when I

had a very strange sensation. I didn't need the *What to Expect When You're Expecting* book to tell me what it was. I *knew*. I was in labor. AGAIN. I was shocked. I grabbed the Hubs's arm as a painful contraction took hold of me. "Something is not right!" I gasped.

"What's wrong?" The Hubs looked panicked.

"I don't know, but I feel like I'm having contractions again." Another one stopped me in my tracks in the middle of the hallway. "Oh my God! What the hell?"

The Hubs helped me back to my room and the contractions got much stronger and suddenly I had a familiar sensation I'd felt just a few days earlier. I needed to *push*! I didn't know what to do. I didn't know where to go.

It was clear that whatever was coming was *not* normal, but I couldn't stop it.

"Holy shit!" I cried. "I'm giving birth to...*something*!" I fell to my knees. I felt my body contract and something smaller than a baby but bigger than a softball exited my body and landed on the floor beneath me. I was afraid to peek under my gown.

"What happened?" the Hubs asked. "Is it out?"

It was out, but whatever it was was still attached *inside* me. I could feel it tug on me every time I shifted. *What the actual fuck???*

"It's out. Sort of," I replied. I finally took a peek between my legs, but I couldn't tell what the hell I was looking at.

"What is it, Jen?" The Hubs was freaking out.

"I don't know."

"Is it another baby?"

"No, I don't think so." I stood up and showed the Hubs. The poor Hubs. He can never bleach his eyeballs enough. I still can't believe he stayed married to me after what he saw.

Swinging between my legs was a mass that looked like that thing from *Alien* that bursts through that guy's chest, only this one looked like it broke out of my vagina and was swinging from a vine.

"Holy shit!" The Hubs gagged and tried to avert his eyes.

"Get. The. Goddamn. Nurse," I said.

I didn't have to tell him twice. He ran to the nurses' station, screaming the whole way.

A perky nurse came in with a fake smile plastered on her face and said, "Hi there! I understand you've got a little situation in here. Why don't you hop up on the bed so we can take a look, hon?"

I stood up and showed her my "situation."

She was a consummate professional; her smile only wavered for a second before she composed herself again. "Okay! Well that *is* something, isn't it? Super! Huh. Right. Can I just...see...that again?" I lifted my gown and she nodded. "Okay. I'm just going to go and get my supervisor to take a look at...um...that...and she's going to know *exactly* what to do. We're going to get you fixed up in no time!" She gulped and got out of there fast.

Now I was crying. "What is it??" I asked the Hubs.

"I have no idea, but it's disgusting, whatever it is."

*Thanks, Hubs. I wasn't sure.*

The supervisor, the perky nurse, and a couple of backups came in. This was obviously a real teaching moment, because whatever the hell was between my legs was something none of them had ever seen up close and personal. The supervisor got me on the bed where she could inspect me, trying to hide the fear and horror in her eyes. "Well, I think we should go ahead and massage your stomach. That might make it evacuate your body completely," she tried.

"It's attached," I hissed. "I can *feel* it. I need a doctor."

After a small powwow they decided that no amount of massaging was going to make this thing disengage and the best thing was for me to be readmitted to the hospital.

They trundled me into a wheelchair and suddenly became very, very busy. I was no longer their problem. They pointed the Hubs in the general direction of the Emergency Room and pulled out copious amounts of paperwork to bury themselves under so they would never have to see me and the medical waste between my legs ever again. The look of relief on all their faces as the Hubs wheeled me down the hall confirmed to me that they had no clue what the hell was hanging between my legs.

We got to the ER and a receptionist started to SLOWLY take our info while I sobbed quietly and tried to sit carefully in the wheelchair so as not to squish the mass.

The Hubs said, "She's a boarder, but she was just discharged today. Surely you can just look her up rather than us giving you all this info again. She needs to see someone. She's got a...situation."

"Sir, I need to do my job first and then you can see the doctor. Now ma'am, tell me what exactly is the problem."

I'd had it. I couldn't half sit on a warm, pulsing (yeah, it was fucking pulsing!) mass any longer while this dumb bitch typed in my home phone number with one finger. "I have a softball-sized ball of God knows what dangling between my legs. It smells like death, it looks like hell, and I need a doctor right now unless *you'd* like to take a crack at it! Do your fucking job!"

What do you know? That bitch did her job and she found me in the system.

They put me and Gomer's Twin—I'd decided that this was Gomer's twin that he'd somehow consumed in the womb, leaving this tiny carcass inside my body as a warning to any siblings that might try and follow in his wake—into a waiting room.

I was really blubbering now. The fear and exhaustion were getting to me and I was starting to lose it. "What time is it?" I whispered to the Hubs.

"I don't know." He looked at his watch. "It's two."

"In the morning or the afternoon?" I asked.

Have you ever noticed that hospitals are a bit like casinos? There were no windows in the NICU and I'd been living in a storage closet that didn't have a window. (Truly, I was staying in a closet. My room had a bed, a bathroom, and dozens of medical-grade breast pumps lined up along the walls—even in there those motherfuckers were taunting me: "*Still no milk, Jen?*") I'd long ago lost track of whether it was day or night. Everywhere I went in the hospital, lights blazed overhead and the staff hurried about as if it was always ten a.m.

"Two in the morning," the Hubs said.

The door to my room opened and in walked the lucky emergency room doctor who drew my file. She said, "Hello, Jen, I'm—"

"Finally!" I interrupted her. I was so happy to see her. "Oh my God! I'm so glad you're here. You can help me. You can fix me. You can tell me what this is," I blathered, clawing for her hand.

"Dr. Simpson," she finished. The startled doctor took a closer look and finally saw the three-day-old bedhead, the wild eyes, and the grungy hospital gown. She probably thought I was there looking for pain pills or something. "Wow. You look...wow. Okay, so what's going on?"

*"This!"* I said and dramatically whipped back the sheet that was covering me and Gomer's Twin. Again, I got *barely* a flinch. Damn, those medical professionals were good at hiding surprise and/or disgust!

"Uh-huh," Dr. Simpson said, moving in close to examine the Twin. "I see," she said, taking it in from another angle. "I got it."

"You got it? You know what it is?" I asked excitedly.

"Oh! Yeah, no, not really. I've never seen anything like it. Maybe in a textbook once."

"I think it's Gomer's Twin! I think he ate it!" I said crazily.

*"Riiiight.* Hold on, I'm going to try something." She yanked on Gomer's Twin and I gasped in pain and resisted the urge to kick her in the head. "Yeah, that's not going to work."

*No shit, doc. Did you learn that move in med school?*

"Okay, I'm going to need to get an O.B. in here to consult with me, because I don't...this isn't...really my area."

Luckily, my O.B was on call that night/morning. He arrived looking fresh as a daisy for two a.m. and had Dr. Simpson in tow.

I flung back my sheet and waited for the micro-flinch, but it never came. This guy had obviously seen everything and anything come out of a hooha!

"I'm not a hundred percent positive, but I'm pretty sure it's an additional placenta lobe," he said.

"That's what I thought," Dr. Simpson said with a smile, giving herself a virtual pat on the back. "But I wanted to be sure."

"Not Gomer's Twin? I think it's his twin. He killed it and left it as a warning!"

"Jen, it's not a twin. Obviously, we'll send it to pathology and have it biopsied to confirm, but I'm sure it's an extra placenta that the midwife missed. I've just never seen one so large," he went on.

An *extra* placenta? Extra as in more? Bigger? Better? Hang on. My body had created an extra placenta!? Oh yeah! This was obviously a sign that I was an awesome mother! That I kicked ass at my new job. I didn't just make one placenta like any average mother! I made two! Suck it, losers who only make one placenta. I couldn't wait to walk back into the NICU and demand the nursing chair for me and my overachieving uterus.

"You haven't had any heavy bleeding, Jen?"

"No, the nurses checked and said it was normal."

"No discomfort?" my doctor asked.

"Yes, lots of discomfort. I've been telling them for days that I felt like hell. My back hurt, I had cramps, and I've been really weak. They told me it was normal, because I'm too old for this job."

"Uh-huh." Now I could see the micro-flinch. The nurses had totally fucked up their jobs. "Is your milk in?"

"No. Not yet." Wow, was he judging me for not breast-feeding too? It didn't even phase me because I was killing it in the uterus department.

"Did you tell the nurses?" Dr. Simpson asked.

"I told anyone who would listen. The lactation consultant has been working with me for a couple days trying to wring whatever she can from my boobs. It's been like trying to get blood from a stone."

Ha! More flinching! They couldn't hide it that time. The two doctors even exchanged a look.

I've since discovered that leftover placenta is a potential killer. Women can bleed to death if not treated. While I didn't have excessive bleeding, I did have other telltale symptoms like my milk not coming in and I wasn't bouncing back as quickly as I was supposed to. And SOMEONE should have noticed that I was more than just a fucking complainer! I didn't suck at my job—they sucked at theirs!

I didn't care, though, at that point. I just wanted Gomer's Twin gone. "How can you get this thing out of me?" I squeaked.

"We'll have to operate," the doctor said simply. "And quickly. It needs to come out right away."

The next day I was a full-fledged patient again, recovering from emergency surgery. I woke up feeling surprisingly well. I was still weak and emotional, but the back pain was gone. I was contemplating a visit to the NICU when my phone rang. It was my client Bob. The one I'd rescheduled earlier in the week. I tried to do the math and determined that it was Friday, Bob's new closing date.

"Hi, Bob," I said.

"I haven't heard from you," Bob said. "Are you coming to my closing today?"

"No, I'm sorry. I can't make it. Let me call my associate Jonathan. I had him on my backup list and he can be there with you."

"What if there are any last-minute snags?" Bob asked petulantly.

I closed my eyes and tried not to scream. Last-minute snags? On a simple transaction that closing companies do every single day? "Bob, I don't anticipate any snags. The sellers have already signed and moved out. Your loan is approved. You just need to sign the documents and take the keys. That's it."

"But what if something comes up? I probably won't be able to reach you."

"No," I agreed. "That's why you have Jonathan. He's

taking over all of my business for the next few days. I'm going to call him right now and Jonathan will be at your closing."

"I don't know Jonathan," Bob said.

"He's a good guy. He's been handling all of my files this week while I'm out on maternity leave."

"But didn't you have your baby earlier this week? Couldn't you come for an hour? You said you'd be there."

"I know I did. That was stupid of me," I said. "I didn't realize how much work it is to take care of an infant. In fact, we're still in the hospital, Bob." I didn't really want to get into the details with Bob and I hoped that would suffice and that he'd back the fuck off.

"At some point you will have to figure out how to balance your work with your baby. You might as well start now, don't you think?"

I was stunned. What a dick. I sat there in silence. I just kept thinking about Gomer in his little Isolette and this asshole who wanted me to leave "just for an hour" so I could watch him sign some fucking papers. "I'm sorry, Bob," I said through gritted teeth, "but I can't come today."

"Well, I'll have to think long and hard before I ever recommend you to any of my friends in the future."

"You do what you have to do," I replied, tears running down my face. *Dickhead, motherfucking piece of shit, asshole...*

At that very moment my friend Karen walked in the door. Karen was my mom's age and she'd been doing the mother job for many years at that point. As soon as she saw me crying, she went into Mama Bear mode. "What's happening, Jen?" she asked. "Is it Gomer?"

I shook my head and pointed to the phone. "It's my client. He's upset with me," I said.

Karen snatched the phone from my hand. "Hello? Who is this? Well, this is Jen's friend, Karen. Listen here, I don't know what you're complaining about and I really don't care. Do you have any clue what Jen has been through in the last few days? She has a very sick, very tiny baby in the NICU. She's recovering from emergency surgery. And then I walk in here and she's crying. Why are you making her cry?" Karen listened silently for a few moments and then said, "Well, Bob, you're a man who has no idea what's going on right now, so I'm going to give you a lesson. This job—taking care of Gomer—is the most important job Jen has now. Do you have a mother? Call your mother when I'm done and she'll verify all of this. There is no way that any woman who has been through what Jen has been through in the last few days will drag herself out of the hospital and away from her tiny baby to come to your stupid closing! Your closing! Do you hear yourself? You're mad because Jen won't be there when you sign some papers. Yes, I understand it's a big moment for you, but JEN JUST HAD A BABY! That's a big moment too! You're a big boy, you can handle it by yourself. And if you don't think you can, then reschedule your closing for a month from now when Jen is feeling better!" And then she snapped my flip phone closed.

"That was amazing, Karen!" I said, sniffling. "Thank you!"

Karen shrugged. "Well, he's never going to refer you to anyone."

Karen was right. I never heard from Bob or any of his friends again. But Karen was also right about something else. Gomer was my most important job. I was going to have to figure out how to balance my work and caring for him, but he would always be the priority going forward. It was a new job for me, and it was one I was going to have for life.

## CHAPTER 13

### "HEY MAN, DO YOU THINK I'M DOING THIS FOR MY HEALTH?" AND OTHER THINGS I'D LIKE TO YELL AT PEOPLE

I WOULD LIKE to think that I'm very hip and with-it, but as I've aged I've realized that I'm quickly becoming the old lady who comes out of her house in her dingy bathrobe to yell at the kids to get off her lawn. Oh, who am I kidding? I've never been hip and with-it and I've always enjoyed yelling at the neighbor kids.

I have always been reluctant to embrace new technology. I still remember the day in the late nineties when my boss told me about a smartphone he'd seen. He described the tiny screen and told me that someday I would answer emails and watch movies on my phone. My response was, "Why would I ever want to watch a movie on such a tiny screen?" (That day I should have invested every penny I had into whatever company made that smartphone, because right now I am thinking about watching a movie on my phone instead of telling you this story. Stupid me.) I carried a cellphone—it was one of those old bricks with the built-in antenna you see in old-timey movies, kids. It was for emergencies only and half the time I left it sitting on the charger back at my house because I forgot to grab it on the way out the door.

When I started selling real estate in 2002, I had embraced the cellphone a bit more because I liked the idea of having a virtual office. It was my first taste of the freedom technology could afford me. I could sit at home in my PJs or by the pool on vacation and it didn't matter, because when my phone rang I was ready for business. As the years progressed, I found myself working remotely more often than not. Gomer was a baby and I liked working from home or the park. So I let myself be dragged slowly into the digital age.

I got email on my phone when I realized my virtual office would get a lot lighter when I didn't have to lug a diaper bag *and* a laptop everywhere I went. I upgraded to a flip phone because it fit in the cup holder on my stroller perfectly. Technology-wise it was a step up from the brick, and it was hard enough for me to master. I just wanted to make phone calls and answer emails. I had heard other Realtors in my office talk about "texting" but I had no desire to learn more. The idea of scrolling through the alphabet so I could avoid talking on the phone seemed absolutely insane to me. I communicated with my clients a lot over email but only so I could have a record of what was said on our phone calls, because I really preferred to talk to them on the phone. Real estate is all about personal relationships and it can be a tricky business at times, and there's a lot that cannot be inferred through acronyms typed with fat thumbs on an impersonal screen.

One of the ways I found new clients was to team up with my favorite mortgage broker, Silas, and offer free home-buying seminars for first-time buyers. We'd invite a bunch of new, young prospective clients, ply them with food and drink, and then explain why owning a house was the best thing ever if you overlooked leaky roofs or having to clean out gutters.

The seminars were very hit or miss. Sometimes we had a roomful of people and sometimes we had a couple of people. One night we had one lone guy: Charlie.

Charlie showed up early that night. He was first, of course, but we didn't realize he'd be the only one. Silas invited him to fix a plate and find a seat. Charlie fixed two plates. Silas gave me a look and I shrugged. The sandwiches were a couple bucks each. If Charlie bought a house, I'd buy him a platter of sandwiches.

Silas and I tried to chat him up with small talk, but he wasn't having it. "What part of town do you live in now?" I asked.

Charlie shrugged and mumbled something that sounded like "Maple."

"Are you thinking of buying in the next year or so?" Silas asked.

Charlie's mouth was full of food and it sounded like he said "Maple" again. That's when he literally picked up his two plates and moved to another part of the room.

"Message received," Silas whispered in my ear. In Charlie's defense, we pounced on him pretty hard since he was the only person there.

After a few more minutes I realized that no one else was coming. "I guess we should get started, Charlie," I said. He was sitting in the last row. "Do you want to move a bit closer?"

He shook his head.

"Maybe we could just sit down and sort of discuss your specific questions rather than me going through a whole PowerPoint presentation?" I suggested.

"We could really figure out your particular wants and needs," Silas offered.

"I might be repeating stuff you already know," I said.

Charlie balked. "No, I'd like to hear the whole presentation," he said. "If I have questions I'll ask when you're done."

"No problem!" I said cheerfully, but inside I was thinking, *This is going to be weird as fuck.*

"Be sure to stop Jen if she's boring you," Silas teased.

Charlie stared balefully.

"Okay, here we go!" I launched into the first of my thirty slides. I was just moving on to my second slide when I heard a distracting noise.

*Click, click, click, click, click, click.*

I frowned and glanced around the room, trying to decide what was making that annoying noise. I didn't want my new skittish client to run off because of an irritating sound! I caught Silas's eye and gave him a look that said, *What is that?*

He raised an eyebrow and jutted his chin toward Charlie. He was sitting back there with his head down and he was typing away like a madman on his cellphone. *Click, click, click.* His phone vibrated with each keystroke.

*How rude!* I mouthed to Silas. He nodded. I was so angry, but I didn't want Charlie to know. I kept going with my presentation, but all I could think about was Gomer, and Silas's little boy, and how they'd be going to bed that night without a kiss from their parents because we were talking to this guy who couldn't be bothered to put down his phone and listen for an hour! *Are you fucking kidding me,*

*Charlie?* I thought. *Do I look like I enjoy talking to an empty room? Do you not have the common courtesy to get off your fucking phone and at least pretend like what I have to say is interesting?* I gave Silas a look: *What the fuck, man?*

Silas shrugged. *Beats me.*

I stopped speaking and waited to see if Charlie would notice. He looked up, dazed.

"Are you okay back there?" I asked. "Can you hear me all right?" "Yeah," he said, turning his attention back to his phone. "It's fine."

I wanted to throw my shoe at him. I decided to put the presentation into hyper-mode at that point. It was abundantly clear that Charlie was just there for the free food and didn't give a shit about what I was saying. I wasn't going to quit, because I was a fucking professional, but I could definitely hurry through and get the hell out of there in record time. I sped up a bit and so did the *click, click, clicking*. I was so distracted twice I lost my train of thought and ended up either repeating myself or saying "um" about twenty-seven times while I tried to remember where I'd left off.

Finally, I couldn't take it anymore. I said, "Hey Charlie, if you don't want to be here, I get it. I do. But Silas and I are here to help you, and if you don't want our help, you should say so now so that we can all move on. I'd rather have a no than a maybe."

Charlie looked up from his phone, his mouth in an "O."

Silas looked surprised too. He cleared his throat and tried to soften my blow. "I think what Jen is trying to say is if you don't think home-buying is for you, just tell us and we'll let you go. You don't need to stay if this is boring you."

Charlie frowned. "Why would you think I'm bored?"

"Well..." Silas said, motioning to the phone in Charlie's hand.

"You haven't stopped texting since you sat down," I said. "You must be bored. It's very apparent to me and Silas."

Charlie looked at the phone in his hand. "Yeah, I'm texting."

"Exactly!" I said. "It's incredibly rude. You're the only person here. We're doing all of this for you, and you're texting the whole time. We can hear the phone clicking and it's very distracting."

Charlie shrugged. "It's just that my girlfriend was the one who wanted to come to this thing. She couldn't come because she's sick and so I've been texting her everything you've said, Jen."

Now my mouth was an "O."

"You've been texting Jen's whole presentation to your girlfriend?" Silas asked.

"Yeah, I mean, most of it," Charlie said. "The last two slides were really fast, so I'm trying to catch up."

"You have been listening?" I asked, feeling like a complete ass.

"Of course. I told you, this is really important to my girlfriend. She's the one who wants us to buy a house. I don't care one way or another. I probably would have sent her to this thing by herself, but when she got sick I said I'd come and text her. I thought there'd be more people here and so it wouldn't be so noticeable."

"We could call her and put her on speakerphone," I said, motioning to the giant speakerphone at the front of the room.

"It's just that it would be easier for you," Silas said. "I can move the phone right by Jen and your girlfriend won't miss anything and you won't have to type so much."

"Oh God, no!" Charlie said, looking downright ill. "No one wants to, like, be on the phone, you know?"

Silas and I stared at him blankly, because no, we didn't know.

"So, no phone?" I asked one more time.

"No," Charlie said.

I got back to my presentation and Charlie got back to clicking away—I slowed down so he could keep up. At the end, I asked if he had any questions. We had to wait in a super-awkward silence while his girlfriend texted him her questions.

"She wants to know what we can afford," Charlie said.

"That's my area of expertise!" Silas said. "I can get you pre-approved right now, but I have a lot of questions and we'll need to get your girlfriend on the phone."

"Let me see if she wants to talk," Charlie said. He *click, click, clicked.* And we wait, wait, waited. Finally he said, "Okay, she says we can call with the questions."

Silas took Charlie in his office and got all the information he needed.

I went home that night and told the Hubs about our experience. "It's like he thought talking on the phone was the worst thing ever," I said.

The Hubs shrugged. "I'm all for technology, but typing all that stuff out sounds crazy when he could have just conference-called her."

"That's what we said! Silas finally got her to talk on the phone so he could get her personal info and stuff and he said it was painful."

I checked my email on my laptop and I saw two new emails. One was from Charlie telling me he was pre-approved with Silas and wanted to start house shopping as soon as his girlfriend felt better. "I tried to text you tonight, but I don't think you got it," he wrote. "Please text me back, asap, so I know you want to work with us. I will have to text someone else if I don't hear back from you right away."

The second email was from Silas with Charlie's pre-approval letter. The guy could afford a very nice house!

"I need you to show me how to text right this minute!" I yelled, scaring the Hubs.

"What? Why?"

"I have to text this guy right now before he goes with a Realtor who can text!"

"Jen, this can wait until morning," the Hubs said.

"No, it can't! This dude is serious. Show me how to text right now."

"On your crappy little phone? It will take you ages to text him. We'll get you a new plan and a new phone."

"I don't care. Just show me how to do it, please."

The Hubs gave me a lesson, and within a few minutes I was scrolling and pecking a message on my phone:

*Hello, Charlie. I received your email and pre-approval letter. Thank you. I will call you tomorrow to see how your girlfriend is feeling and set up a time we can look at houses together.*

Charlie texted back immediately:

*NO CALLS.*

By the end of the week Charlie and his girlfriend, Casey, were out looking at houses. They had referred me to two other phone-adverse clients, so I had a shiny new phone with a full keyboard that I was trying to learn to use before it became obsolete and I would be left in the Dark Ages once again.

It still goes that way for me. It's 2017 and I finally just started a Snapchat account this week only so I can keep tabs on Gomer and see what he's up to. When he showed me the filters I said, "Gomer, I don't want to make myself into a sexy deer! I am forty-five years old. This is so stupid!" And then he showed me the filter and I was like, "Oooh, I look kind of cute, yeah? Quick, make me a sexy puppy!"

# CHAPTER 14

## THIS IS GOING TO BE GREAT OR WE'RE GOING TO GET DIVORCED

WHEN I WAS eight and a half months pregnant with Adolpha, the Hubs was fired from his job. He was told that he didn't fit in with the "corporate culture." There isn't a lot you can say when this is the reason you're given for being fired. He'd done a good job and he'd had success, but he just didn't fit in. And he didn't fit in for good reason. He wasn't a fratboy bro. He didn't drink the (spiked) Kool-Aid and join the group of lemmings sacrificing their lives and marriages for The Company. The Hubs had a toddler and a pregnant wife at home and so he didn't accept a lot of invitations to hang out at the bar or play on the corporate softball league. The Hubs has always been a loner by nature and in the past that had never been a problem. But this time it was. He was just too damn old and square to fit in and so they let him go.

When I'd gone into pre-term labor with Gomer I was told it was stress-related, so when the Hubs told me the news, I was shocked, but I was even more shocked when contractions didn't begin immediately. "I can't believe those assholes fired you!" I yelled. "They just saw me at the family fucking Oktoberfest thing. Your boss asked me when

I was due! How could they fire a man with a pregnant wife? I will burn that place to the ground!"

"It's okay, I have an idea, Jen," the Hubs reassured me.

I waited for him to say, "I'm going to send out a billion resumes first thing tomorrow morning." Instead he said, "I'm going to go to work with you."

"I'm sorry, what did you say?" I said. Adolpha did a flip-flop in my belly and I felt my lunch threaten to make an appearance. "What are you even talking about?"

"Just hear me out," the Hubs said. "Whoa. Sit down, Jen, you don't look so good. We can't afford for you to go into pre-term labor again this time. We're on COBRA and that shit's expensive. You need to clench or something. We need this baby to cook longer."

I sat down. "Explain yourself," I said through gritted teeth. "I'm clenching everything."

"So, this has been coming for a while now. I'm not surprised. I knew I wasn't fitting in and I knew they'd probably let me go sooner rather than later, so I've been looking for a job for the last few months now."

"You have? Why didn't you tell me?"

"I didn't want to worry you. You've got a lot going on and I didn't want to add to your stress."

"You could have told me," I said, instantly calming down and feeling bad that the Hubs had been struggling on his own. "We're a team."

He smiled. "I'm glad you feel that way. See, I've sent out a ton of resumes and I haven't heard back from anyone. Not one company has replied, Jen. Do you know how rare that is? I always get an interview at least. There is something going on."

Oh, the Hubs was absolutely right. Something was going on. It was late 2006 and our country was on the cusp of The Great Recession, but the Hubs and I didn't know that yet. "I'm sure it's just a hiring freeze since we're close to the holidays and the end of the year," I said. "No one hires in October, right?"

"I don't know," the Hubs said. "It's weird. I've been on the internet a lot and everyone's talking about it. Jobs are scarce and applications are way up. And then if you even get an offer, it's a shit offer."

"So what's your plan?" I asked warily.

"Look, you're killing it at real estate, right?" he said, trying to butter me up.

"Sort of," I said. *Killing it* was a strong statement. I'd been selling real estate for four years at that point and every year was a decent year for me. I had a fairly successful real estate career, but that was because I didn't have the pressure to be the breadwinner. The Hubs had the "real job." He was the one who always had a steady salary we could count on. I worked on commission. We planned our budget to live on his income, and what I earned was "mad money." His job gave us benefits and a lot of times he got a car too.

"Jen, you're underestimating yourself."

"No, I'm really not," I said. "I'm trying to balance it all. Real estate is great because I can work with a lot of different people and every day is different. I like being able to work from home and I love that Gomer can go with me a lot of the time." Yeah, Gomer really did go with me. When he was a new baby I put Gomer in one of those Baby Bjorn things and he was my coworker. No one minded him tagging along because he was such a good baby. But I'd cut back significantly on my networking since he'd been born. All of my clients were coming from referrals from past clients or the Kindermusik class Gomer and I attended each week. I wasn't doing a lot to fill my pipeline.

"Just the other day you said you have more clients than you can handle. That you're too busy."

"Well, that's mostly because I'm exhausted. Gomer's getting too big to lug around and Adolpha is sucking the life out of me—literally. She makes me sick every single day. Yesterday I was out showing houses to the McMillans and I had to pull the car over so I could puke on the side of the road. Not my finest moment. Luckily they were cool about it."

"Exactly. You can barely manage your workload and Gomer, but soon the baby will be here and how are you going to handle that? You can't take a baby and a toddler with you everywhere."

What was he saying? "So you want to be the manny?" I asked.

"No!" the Hubs said. "I want to be your associate. I want to be a Realtor."

"I need help, but I don't have enough clients for the both of us. That's what I'm telling you. I have slacked off with my networking. We need more clients if you're going to join me."

"Your client list hasn't stopped growing, but I can help you grow it faster. The real estate market is booming."

This is when it would have been great to have a crystal ball to see into the future. This is when it would have been nice to look ahead and see the upcoming housing bubble burst that would implode into a billion pieces. "I do have a lot of listings," I conceded. Of course I had a lot of listings—tons of people were trying to sell their homes before the banks took them away. "What are you proposing?" I asked.

"Instead of hiring some loser who won't do the work right, you should hire me!"

"I don't know," I said, feeling nauseated. I didn't know if it was Adolpha or the Hubs making me feel so sick.

"It's going to be great!" the Hubs promised. "I'll still send out resumes and go on interviews—if anyone calls me —but I'll be able to help you out. No one will work for you as hard as me."

"That's true," I agreed.

"And whether you like it or not, you were going to have to hire someone after Adolpha is born. If you give me the job, you can keep the money in the family."

"I'd feel better if you had a real job though," I said. "What about insurance and stuff?"

The Hubs waved a hand. "Meh. We'll figure out all of that down the road."

"This is what you want to do?"

"Yes!" the Hubs said emphatically. "And we'll be together. All the time!"

I tried to make my smile look less terrified. "Yay," I said.

"This is going to be great!" the Hubs said, pumping his fist in the air.

"Or we're going to get divorced," I said.

He stopped with the fist-pumping and stared at me. "Why would you even say that, Jen?" I shrugged. "I don't know. How many married couples do you know that work together?"

The Hubs was silent.

"Yeah, me neither. Couples should not work together. It's not healthy to be together all the time. It's not normal. Also, we're both bossy, opinionated people who want to be in charge. How is that going to work?"

"Jen, this is your business. I know you've worked hard and built it up and I'm just here to help you," the Hubs said. "In fact, I'll be your bitch."

"My bitch?" I said, surprised. But I also kind of liked the sound of that.

He nodded vigorously. "I'll do all the grunt work. I'll run around and put out signs and pick up contracts. I'll even take care of Gomer. I can't wait to spend more time with him! We'll have so much fun together. And whatever you need me to do. How about this? You're not feeling well and you're out all day with buyers. You should not be puking in bushes. Puke at home. I'll handle the buyers and you handle the listings. Those are easier to do from home. This way you can just focus on selling houses and getting your pregnancy to full-term."

I sighed. "Okay, let's try it," I said.

It wasn't like we had any other choice at that point. No one was calling him, I needed the help, and he was willing to check his ego at the door.

———

That weekend the Hubs had his first opportunity to work for, I mean *with,* me. I had an open house scheduled for Sunday afternoon. He wanted to man the open house and let me stay home.

"I can do it, Jen," he argued. "You stay home, put your feet up, eat some frozen grapes."

"No!" I said, because I couldn't allow that. For one, he wasn't a licensed Realtor and so he could not hold the open house. (I am a stickler for the rules.) And two, what did he know about selling houses? He wasn't ready to be turned loose! But frozen grapes did sound delicious ... No! I couldn't let him do it.

"I really need you to stay home with Gomer," I said. "I'll

be fine. Maybe next time I'll let you do it, but you're not ready yet."

That night I couldn't sleep (thanks for the heartburn, Adolpha) and I was flipping channels on the TV. A story about a murder caught my attention. The victim was nine months pregnant and she answered an ad on Craigslist to buy baby items. The Craigslist Killer (that's what they called her) lured the pregnant woman into the house with promises of cheap Bumbo seats and cloth diapers and then killed her. Only she didn't just kill her, she stole the baby from her womb! Now the whole state was looking for the killer and the baby. I'm sure the fact that I was thirty-six weeks pregnant and prone to hysterical outbursts had nothing to do with the fact that I woke up the Hubs who was slumbering beside me. "I need you!"

He sat straight up in bed, looking around wildly. "What is it? Did your water break? Is the mattress ruined?"

"I'm calling my mother. She'll keep Gomer tomorrow. You're coming with me to the open house."

Once the Hubs determined our mattress was fine, he got excited. "I can? You need me?"

"Yes, I need you there to protect me in case there's a crazy baby snatcher."

He frowned. "A crazy baby snatcher who trolls open houses hoping to come upon a very pregnant Realtor who is all alone in a kitchen full of butcher knives?" he asked.

"YES, exactly! See? It can happen! You just said so."

The Hubs shook his head. "I don't think it happens that way, Jen."

"Do you want to be at the open house or not?" I cried.

He tried to soothe me. "Yes, yes, of course I'll be there. Don't even worry."

The next day we arrived at the house and I sent the

Hubs around to turn on all the lights, straighten the beds, and flush all the toilets (you'd be shocked to know how many people forget to flush their toilets) while I put out the cookies and lit a smelly candle. He was right—having him around *did* make my life easier!

When he joined me in the kitchen again, I noticed that he was wearing his sunglasses. "Put on your real glasses," I said. "You look like a pedophile."

"Yeah, um, that's the thing," he said. "I forgot my glasses at home. We were in such a hurry and I didn't want to forget anything important like the open house signs, but I forgot my glasses. These are all I have."

"Can you try going without glasses?" I asked.

"Are you kidding?" The Hubs has terrible eyesight. Like, super bad. So bad that he can't read the digital clock on the opposite side of our bedroom bad. He can't be without glasses and he doesn't wear contacts.

"Shit," I said. "What are we going to do? I'm not even kidding. You look like a weirdo in those things when you're outside, but inside takes it to a whole new level of creeper."

"I know what I can do!" the Hubs said. "I'll just pretend like I'm a looky-loo. I'll walk around the house and say stuff like, 'Wow, this closet is *ah-may-zing*. I've never seen one so spacious before.' Or I could hang out in the backyard and talk about the roof. I'll be a plant. It will actually work better, because no one trusts what the Realtor says, but they'll trust—"

"A random dude talking to himself at an open house?" I asked.

He couldn't respond, because at that moment the door opened and my first prospective client walked in. "Hello? Are you open?" the man called.

"Yes! Come on in!" I called back. I hissed at the Hubs, "Go! Go! Admire the closets or some shit."

For the next hour the Hubs wandered around the house with potential buyers and pointed out things that an ordinary home buyer would not notice. "I think this water heater looks new. I bet it's less than six months old. Forget stainless appliances, now *that's* a feature!"

Everyone was looking slightly uncomfortable when they left the house and no one made an offer. I was thinking of closing up early when two women wandered in. They arrived a few minutes apart, so I could tell they weren't together, but they were both visibly pregnant. In sales you always try to find something you have in common so you can bond over shared interests. The pregnant thing seemed like an easy one, but pregnant ladies are skittish on good days. Half the time you can't be certain a woman is pregnant, and even if you are and she is, chances are high that you'll offend her when you ask when she's due. You can't touch her belly because that's freaky. You can't ask the gender because that's private. You can't ask if they have a name, because they're sure you're trying to steal it or make fun of it. The three of us could maybe bond over the parasites residing in our abdomens, but ultimately it's best to treat pregnant ladies like they're not even pregnant. And I could bet that they'd both seen the news story about the dead pregnant lady, so their Spidey Senses were tingling even before the Hubs burst out of the basement.

I had no idea what he was doing down there or how long he'd been down there, but suddenly a hyperactive Chinese guy wearing dark glasses and a deranged smile charged from the basement door. "Oh my gosh, I love this house!" he announced to the room. "It's perfect for a family!"

The two women eyed him warily and gave him some space. I tried to call him off with a look and an imperceptible shake of my head, but I think his polarized lenses were clouding his vision.

He continued. "Speaking of family...look at the three of you!"

"Thank you for coming by, sir," I said, giving him a look that said, *Shut the fuck up, already.* "Please call my office if you have any questions."

"Oh, I have a question," the Hubs said, ignoring my signals completely. "Did the three of you plan this? You're all soooo pregnant. You should form a playgroup or something!"

None of us spoke. We all just stared at him. Even I didn't know what to say.

"When are you due?" he asked the one closest to him. "You look like that baby is ready to come out. *Mama, mama! Let me out of here!*" he said in a high-pitched baby voice.

Have you ever seen a woman who is nine months pregnant sprint? I have. It was not a pretty sight. That woman was like a locomotive barreling out of the house. The Hubs stared after her, his mouth hanging open.

I looked at the other woman, waiting for her to bolt too, but she was rooted to her spot. It was like she was paralyzed with fear. And I didn't blame her. The Hubs was fucking terrifying.

I know I should have spoken up at that point. I should have explained to this woman that the horrifying man sending chills down her spine was really my husband who was trying to forge a common bond between us. I should have told her that he sucks at small talk and has no filter, but he's not a serial killer intent on collecting newborns from their wombs. I should have helped her understand that we were still ironing out the kinks of working together. I should have said that I thought the idea of having a plant walk around the house didn't seem like a bad one when it was first proposed to me but now I could see the potential problems. But I didn't say any of those things, because I was like, *I can close her. I have a baby coming and a husband out of work. I need the money and she needs this house.* Because I'm an idiot.

So I ignored the Hubs entirely and said, "Excuse me, ma'am, have you seen the basement?"

The woman glanced at the basement door. "The basement?"

"It's quite spacious. And very quiet," I said, in a way that I felt was not at all like a serial killer and very much like a Realtor trying to point out the benefits of having a place where you can send the kids to play and not hear them fight with one another. "You should see it," I said, moving closer to her.

"What?" she said, clearly alarmed.

I reached out toward her, completely missing the fact that her face was white with terror.

The Hubs yanked off his glasses and stepped between us. "Thank you for coming by," he said, handing the frightened woman my card. "Please let Jen know if you have any questions about the house."

"Why did you do that?" I demanded as I watched the woman waddle full-speed across the street.

"Jen, she's a nosybody. She lives across the street. She's never going to buy this house, but...she might have called the police if we kept talking."

"Good point," I said. "You know, I thought the worst thing about us working together would be we'd get divorced. I never thought it would be that we'd end up in jail."

## CHAPTER 15

### HEY LADY, YOU WISH YOU HAD ANYTHING NICE ENOUGH TO STEAL

"TELL us why we should choose you as our Realtor, Jen," said Clarence.

I was at a listing presentation with Clarence and Doris. Doris and I were in a book club together and she'd mentioned the night before that her husband, Clarence, had accepted a job transfer so they needed to sell their house.

"Do you have a Realtor yet?" I'd asked.

"We're interviewing three tomorrow," Doris had said. "If you want, we can make an appointment with you. I always forget you're a Realtor."

"Really? You forget?" I'd asked.

"No, because you only mention it all the time," Doris said. And she wasn't teasing or anything, she was just being a dick. I didn't care though. I wanted a shot at her listing.

I'd never met Clarence before, but it was clear he was the boss. Doris had barely said a word since I'd arrived.

"Well, I think you should choose me because..." And then I launched into my spiel about why I was the best choice because I'm hardworking, dedicated, experienced, blah, blah, blah.

It was a good thing my speech was memorized or else I would have flubbed it because my head was not in the game. All I could focus on was the fact that the three of us were sitting in the living room together, only Clarence and Doris were sitting at my feet, crisscross style. Oh, and they were dressed identically. When I say identically, I mean *identically*. They were both wearing baggy gray sweatpants, white short-sleeved t-shirts, and thick white athletic socks. The fact that they chose to sit on the floor was unnerving enough, but once I realized they were dressed alike, I couldn't think about anything else.

I was bragging about my final sales price to list price ratio when I couldn't take it anymore. I stopped midsentence and said, "I'm sorry, but wouldn't you both be more comfortable on chairs? I feel sort of strange sitting here on the couch while you're both on the floor." I looked around the room. There were plenty of seats available. It wasn't like I'd taken the only one.

Doris shook her head. "No, we're fine."

"We always sit on the floor," Clarence said.

"You do?" I asked.

"Yes, it's bad for furniture if you sit on it," he said.

Doris chimed in, "Furniture is a big investment and it won't last if you abuse it. Right, Clarence?"

"Right," Clarence confirmed. Yup, he was totally the boss around that house.

"Of course," I said. I couldn't argue with his frugal ways. After all, I lived with a man who whipped out a "buy one, get one" coupon on our first date, and who insisted on all sorts of money-saving techniques like sitting in the dark or unplugging the microwave when it's not in use or keeping twenty-year-old "new" tennis shoes in his closet because he hadn't worn out his current pair yet (spoiler alert: tennis shoes don't last twenty years; the glue breaks down and they literally fall apart in the box). "So you never sit on the furniture?"

He shrugged. "Rarely. We like to keep it nice. This way the cushions never get worn down."

"But who are you saving it for?" I asked. "I mean, if you can't sit on it, who are you keeping it nice for?"

"Company," Doris said. The "duh" was silent.

"Right," I said. "Do you do a lot of entertaining?"

"No, we don't like to socialize much," Clarence said.

"I see." I looked at their matching outfits. I knew there had to be a logic there too and I was dying to find out. I knew I was risking losing the listing, but I couldn't stop myself. I went for it. "So, why do you both dress alike?"

Doris giggled. "We only do this when we aren't going to see anyone important."

I tried not to let her words sting, but *Ow! Not important? Me?*

Clarence continued. "It's just easier. We're the same size in sweatpants, t-shirts, and socks so we bought a bunch of them at Sam's Club and we like to wear them when we're home by ourselves. Makes laundry and storing our clothes so much simpler. We both have a few clothes for work and such that are our 'own' but we share our 'home uniforms.'"

I tried to keep my face neutral and pretend like what he said didn't sound like complete insanity. *Holy fucking shit,* I thought. *I can never tell the Hubs about this because he'll want to do it!* "So smart!" I gushed.

After that, I went on to wow them with my unique marketing plan and then we called it a night.

Doris walked me to the door. "We'll let you know, Jen," she said. "Oh, and please don't tell the book club about Clarence and I dressing alike."

The book club was a fairly nice bunch of women, but Doris didn't really fit in. She always complained about the books we chose ("Too much sex" and "I couldn't get past the first chapter" were her favorite go-to put-downs. I don't think she liked one book we chose. The rumor was she couldn't read and she didn't want anyone to know.) and she always brought weird food to share ("I found a recipe for Jell-O with tuna and vegetables in my mother's cookbook. I thought it sounded perfect for tonight."). Basically, Doris had a hard enough time, and she didn't need the book club to know that she and her husband shared a wardrobe. "Of course not," I assured her.

As soon as I got in my car, my phone rang. It was Louise. She was also a member of the book club and lived down the street from Doris. She must have been watching for me. "Were you allowed to sit on the couch?" Louise asked.

"Yes," I said. "How do you know about that?"

"Everyone in the neighborhood knows about that. They had a birthday party for one of their kids and wouldn't let anyone sit on the furniture. Can you imagine? Twenty grown-ass adults sitting on the floor. So fucking nuts. It was all anyone could talk about for months after that."

"They're keeping it nice," I said, kind of defensively. Sure, I thought it was weird as hell, but I felt bad for Doris.

"Did she talk about her frog?" Louise asked.

"Her frog?" I didn't see any pets when I took the tour of the house.

"The cement frog. She keeps it in the backyard now because neighbor kids were stealing it."

"Why did they steal it?"

"She kept it in the front yard and she dressed it up in special tiny clothes. It bugged the shit out of everyone. This is a nice neighborhood. You can't have that ugly shit in your yard. No one wants to see your stupid fucking frog dressed up for the Fourth of July. It started out with the Bunko ladies. They always get so drunk and walk home. They'd dare one another to steal the frog. It would always turn up at the school, or once it was at the bottom of the neighborhood pool. Twice it ended up on the roof of my house."

"Wow, that's kind of mean," I said.

"Seriously?" Louise sounded surprised. "Jen, come on, you're not that nice. If you had to drive past that frog every day you'd do even worse to it. Plus, it's bizarre that she's spent more on clothes for a lawn ornament than she spends on her own clothes. You know she shares clothes from Sam's with her husband, right?"

I tried to feign innocence. "They do?"

"Jen, it's not a secret," Louise said. "They do yard work in their matching sweats. They look like prisoners or something. Are you telling me they weren't dressed alike?"

I sighed. "Yes, they were dressed the same tonight. It was odd."

"Jen, I told you already. Doris is odd."

"I know, but it's a good listing. I think I can sell it fairly quickly. Like you said, this is a nice neighborhood."

"Clarence is going to want too much. He doesn't realize his location is shitty."

Louise was right. Doris's house backed up to a very busy thoroughfare and there was a lot of traffic noise. Clarence had already been hinting at his dream list price which was several thousand more than I had in mind. "I know, but everyone thinks their house is worth more than it actually is. I'm used to dealing with that. I'm not too worried. I can handle Clarence's expectations."

"Well, then what are you worried about?"

I thought for a moment. "Nothing, really. Just that they're lunatics or something. The best part about this job is I get to pick and choose who to work with. Every now and again, I choose poorly," I said, thinking about Bob, the asshole who insisted I drag my postpartum ass to his closing. "But I've been doing so much better lately. They're odd, but I think I can work with odd. I just can't work with crazy town."

Louise laughed. "Oh, they're crazy town," she warned me.

"I think Doris is just misunderstood. She needs a friend. Someone who is nice to her instead of someone who mocks her and steals her frog. I can be her friend," I said.

"Let me know how that goes," Louise said, her voice dripping with sarcasm.

———

A few days later I was standing in Doris's kitchen. She and Clarence had chosen me to list their house and I was there to get signatures on the listing agreement. "I'm so pleased you picked me, Doris," I said.

"Yeah, well, we actually chose another guy but he didn't even return our call when I left a message telling him we chose him, and the other woman told me my furniture sucked and it wouldn't photograph well. What's wrong with my furniture? It's in perfect condition. I don't know. You were available, I guess. So..."

"Umm, great," I said, feeling like an absolute loser. "I guess that's good, though, right?"

She shrugged. "I guess so. Just hurry up and sell this house so I can get out of this town. I hate it here."

Doris hated living in Kansas City. She'd moved from

Austin. She hated Austin too. And Charlotte before that. Basically, Doris hated her whole life. As someone who can see the negative in everything, I sympathized with Doris, but even I was not as bleak as she was. Doris could find the negative in just about everything.

*"Hey Doris, the sun is out!"*

*"We're all going to get melanoma and die!"*

*"Hey Doris, you just gave birth to a beautiful healthy baby!"* *"My vagina will never be the same and this baby's head looks like a cauliflower."*

In short, Doris was a pain-in-the-ass downer, but I figured I could get Clarence to price the house right, sell it in three weeks, ship Doris out of state, collect my check, and never think about her again. Done and done.

Sure enough, a few days later we got an offer on the house. It was low, but it was a good starting point and we negotiated a bit back and forth to get the buyers to come up. I know that clients can get overwhelmed during the negotiations and sometimes they forget all the details. And so that's why we always talk it out and then I send out emails to everyone reconfirming everything they've agreed to and asking them to look over all the documents before they sign anything. I don't remember the particulars of Doris's house, except one thing. On the final round of negotiations the prospective buyers asked Doris and Clarence to throw their playset into the deal. They had a wooden playset in the backyard and when I did the final walkthrough of the property I had asked, "What's going on with the playset? Does it stay or does it go?" Those playsets are worth a couple grand new and many people either take them with them to the new house or they resell them online. An equal number of people don't give a shit about their playsets and are happy to throw them into the pot to sweeten the deal. I remember that Doris and Clarence weren't crazy about throwing in the playset.

"Were you planning on taking it with you?" I asked.

Clarence shrugged. "We hadn't thought about it. Maybe? The movers say I have to take it apart first and that sucks."

"Sometimes people sell them," I suggested. "Did you want to sell it?"

Doris frowned. "You mean like online or whatever? I don't want strangers from the internet coming to my door. Bunch of freaks seeing where we live." She shuddered.

"So, then you want to leave it?" I asked. "Include it in the sale? You've got the price and close date you wanted. If you give them the playset, it's done."

They both pondered my question. Finally Clarence spoke, "Didn't you say you wanted to buy it?"

At the listing appointment I'd asked if it was for sale. I was looking for a playset for my own kids and I thought that maybe Clarence and Doris would be looking to offload theirs for cheap. At the time I was told it was not for sale, and on closer inspection I decided that was fine, because their playset was actually a piece of shit. Those two were worried about their couches, but they clearly didn't care one whit about the playset. Half the rungs on the ladder were missing and the slide had a giant crack down the center. The swings looked rotted.

"It just needs a new coat of stain," Clarence had assured me.

"Umm, I briefly thought about it," I said. "But we decided to buy new instead."

"Really? When did you get it?" Doris asked.

"It's on order. It's coming next week," I replied.

"I see," Doris said, perturbed.

"You said yours wasn't for sale," I reminded her. "And we couldn't find a used one in good shape, so we decided we'd rather have new."

"I kind of thought you were going to buy it," Doris said.

"Well I'm sorry if you got that impression. That wasn't my intention," I said, getting perturbed myself. *What the fuck, lady? You have a good offer and all they want is your shitty playset. Throw it in!*

"That's too bad," Clarence said. "I don't know what we're going to do with it now."

I nudged them back to the matter at hand. "Well, as I said, you have the price and the closing date you were looking for. It's just the playset holding up the deal. You could include it in the contract," I suggested. "You've got all of your terms and you really don't want to mess with the playset."

"I don't know," Clarence said. "I think they should pay for it. How much could I sell it for?"

"I'm not sure. I sell houses, not playsets," I replied.

"Well, you've been looking," Doris said. "What do you think it's worth?" I shrugged. "A few hundred dollars?"

"I feel like if we give it to them, we've lost," said Clarence. "Don't you, Jen?"

This was a common emotion I'd seen a lot with my male clients. Many times I feel like there needs to be a portion of the contract where all the men can measure their penises so we can really see what we're dealing with. It was five hundred dollars worth of wood and rope that Clarence was boohooing over. He was so worried about looking like the tiniest dick in the room that he was risking losing his deal.

"I don't think of it that way, Clarence," I said. "Real estate is always better when everyone feels a little shorted. Your buyer feels like he's losing because he's paying you full price. That's why he wants the playset. He might not even have kids, but wants *something*. Anything to make him feel like you sacrificed too. It's win-win if you give up the playset."

"I don't want win-win," Clarence argued. "I want just win."

I sighed. "Then say no to the playset and see what he does."

"What might he do?" Doris asked, alarmed.

"He might walk."

"Over a playset?" Clarence scoffed. "That's ridiculous."

I shrugged. "Egos are tricky things in real estate, Clarence. I've seen a lot over the years. Right now the ball is in your court. You say yes, give up the playset, the deal is done. We sign papers tonight and you're on your way. You say no, and you give the power back to him and hope he says yes. It's up to you though. I can't make the decision for you."

After much hand-wringing and debating with one another, Doris and Clarence *finally* agreed to leave the playset behind.

"Great!" I said. "You made the right choice."

I wrote up the paperwork, sent my explanatory email to them, and asked them to read the documents before signing. By morning we were on our way to a smooth closing.

About a week later I made a significant change and moved to a different real estate brokerage. I had been negotiating the shift for months and it was finally time to do it. I let all of my clients know I was transitioning offices, but that it would not impact them in the least. Everything would stay the same.

The next day my brand-new boss called me. "Hi, Jen. It's Albert. Would you please stop by my office later today? I have something I need to discuss with you."

Silly, naive Jen thought that Albert was calling a meeting so that he could welcome me to the new office. I arrived completely unaware that I was going to be blindsided.

"Come on in, Jen," Albert said, ushering me through the doorway. He closed the door firmly behind me. "Have a seat."

I sat.

"We've had a very serious allegation leveled against you today, Jen, and I wanted to bring you in here so that we could talk about it," he said.

My stomach bottomed out. "What? What are you talking about?" I said. "What sort of allegation?"

"Now, you're new here and I don't know you very well yet, and so I need to get to the bottom of this before we can proceed."

"What's happened?" I asked, racking my brain. I'm a fairly up-and-up kind of person and so I couldn't imagine what sort of accusation had been thrown my way. *Was I driving too recklessly the other day when I had that family in my car?* I thought. *I was late to that listing appointment last week because I got pulled over for a speeding ticket. Maybe that was it? It has to be my driving! It has to be.* "It's my driving, right?"

Albert looked shocked. "No. No, it has nothing to do with your driving." He sat down behind his desk. "I received a call today from an incredibly upset woman who says she's your client. She says you stole from her."

"I *what?!*"

Albert held up a hand. "She says you hoodwinked her and stole her playset from her. She says that you're a thief and a liar."

Confusion immediately made way for rage. If I could

have thrown a chair through a window at that moment I would have. "Are you fucking kidding me right now?" I yelled. "It's Doris, right?"

Albert nodded. "So this doesn't come as a surprise to you? You knew right away who I was talking about."

"She's the only listing I have with a playset and she thinks that thing is made of solid gold when it's really termite food. I cannot believe she called you and told you all of this. My brand-new boss. She knew I just changed companies this week. That deal was signed and put away a week ago. Why is she doing this now? She's trying to ruin my career!"

"Tell me what happened, Jen. The whole story. Get your file and let's take a look together."

I showed Albert everything, the documents Doris and Clarence had signed, the email correspondence reiterating they had agreed to include their playset in the sale, the handwritten notes I had from our conversation about the playset—all of it. I could barely see straight because I was in an utter rage. My hands were shaking and I was fighting off tears. (I am a rage-crier.) "Do you believe me?" I demanded.

Albert handed back the file. "Yes, I believe you. Honestly, I believed you from the beginning, but I had to make sure there was nothing to her claims."

"How does she think I stole her playset?"

"What she told me was that you told them the new buyers wanted it, but really they didn't and you were going to take it while everyone was at closing."

If I wasn't ready to burn something to the ground right then, I would have laughed. "Like I'm going to sneak over into the backyard and take apart a giant playset, load it up into a truck I don't own, and then drive to my house, and reassemble the thing in my own backyard?"

Albert nodded.

"That's a lot of work for her piece-of-shit playset."

"Well, that's her theory," Albert said.

"So what now?" I asked. "I mean, can she do anything else to me?"

"Besides ruin your reputation? She'll tell everyone in her neighborhood how terrible you are to work with. That's pretty damaging."

I scoffed. "Her whole neighborhood hates her. I'm not afraid of that. She can't go to the police or anything though, right?"

Albert shook his head. "No, it's part of the sale. The documents prove it. Go give her a call and talk her down off the ledge. Try to get her back on your side."

That was probably really good advice, but fuck that noise. I was never going to try and get Doris back on my side. I got in my car and I dialed her number with shaking, rage-filled hands. It went straight to voicemail. Fucking pussy.

"Doris, it's me. I just got out of a meeting with my broker. What the hell, Doris? Why would you do that? What is wrong with you? Call me. You owe me an explanation."

I waited thirty seconds and called again.

"Doris. Me again. I am absolutely enraged right now. I can't believe that you would think that I'd try and steal your stupid fucking shitty playset. What is wrong with you? Are you demented? Call me."

Thirty more seconds passed.

"Doris, for fuck's sake, answer the phone. You were brave this morning when you called my brand-new boss and tried to get my ass fired. Pick up the phone and answer for yourself. You're unbelievable."

My phone immediately pinged with a text message from Doris:

*STOP CALLING ME. YOU'RE SCARING ME.*

Oh my God!!!
I texted back:

*OF COURSE I'M SCARING YOU, BECAUSE YOU'RE A FUCKING CHILD.*

Now, I will admit, this was not my finest moment, but I couldn't even anymore with Doris. All I had ever done was try to help her! She was an outcast everywhere she went. People excluded her and made fun of her and her frog and her style and her Debbie Downer outlook on life. I was the only fucking person who was nice to her. I was the only one who would stick up for her. I was the only one who even tried to help her sell her house with its ugly-ass furniture (yes, that other Realtor was right; that furniture was hideous)! Well, NO MORE. She was dead to me. She had tried to ruin my career. Luckily Albert was a levelheaded boss and I was someone who took detailed notes, otherwise who knows what might have happened?

I called Louise next. "I can't say exactly what's going on, but let's just say that if your Bunko club wanted to T.P. Doris's house, I'd buy the toilet paper."

"Uh-oh," Louise said. "She showed you her crazy side, didn't she?"

"And then some," I said.

"Oh my God! Really? My neighbor said Doris once threw apples at her in the grocery store. Is it apple-throwing crazy?"

"More," I said.

"You want to smash that frog now, don't you?"

"You have no idea."

"What did she have to say for herself?" Louise asked.

"Nothing. She won't speak to me."

"Really? Not at all?"

"She says she's afraid of me. She won't answer her phone. She'll only text."

"Holy shit. What have you done, Jen?"

"Me? I did nothing. Except be far too nice to her."

Louise laughed. "Okay, I'm not sure that's the lesson you're supposed to be learning here."

"Fuck her, fuck Clarence, fuck their matching sweat-pants, fuck their house, and fuck their dog, even."

Louise laughed again. "Oh Jen, I think you need to hang up the phone and do some meditation before you hurt your-self—or someone else."

"No, what I need to do is go and sit in her driveway and wait for her to come out and check the mail."

"You're not going to do that, are you, Jen?" Louise sounded genuinely alarmed.

"She can't avoid me forever," I said. "She'll have to go and get her kids from the bus stop and I'll be there. She owes me an explanation for her behavior."

"Jen, please don't do that. I don't know what's going on between you two, but I can assure you that you stalking her will escalate whatever it is."

"What, am I supposed to be afraid of her? You think she's going to hit me or something? She won't even answer the phone!"

"I'm just saying that right now I'm on your side and it sounds like she did something to deserve this anger, but soon you're going to cross a line and suddenly you'll be the bad guy. You know?"

"Are you saying *I'm* the crazy one now?" I demanded. "Are you calling me crazy, Louise?"

"See? I'm telling you, Jen. Let it go. This is how *Dateline* specials happen." Louise hung up the phone.

Wow. All of a sudden I was the cuckoo. Fucking Doris.

I did not do any meditation that day. Instead I spent the rest of the day waiting for Doris to call me. Which she never did. I did not show up at her closing a few weeks later because I didn't trust myself to be in a room with her and Clarence. I sent someone else to pick up my sign and lockbox from their house. I did not attend her final book club and I blocked her on all social media because her Debbie Downer updates made me want to shoot myself in the face.

And then Louise called me. "Oh. My. God. I heard what happened with Doris," she said.

"How?"

"She went to Bunko and told everyone what you did. Well, what you tried to do—allegedly, or whatever. You tried to steal her playset?"

"You believed her?" I asked, incredulous.

"No, I didn't. A few of the neighbors did, but I defended you."

"Thanks," I said.

"What a random thing to accuse you of," she said.

"I know. She's so fucking deranged."

"Well, don't worry. The moving truck is there today. And...I might have started something."

"What are you talking about?"

"Well, I know I told you to let it go, but then when I heard what she'd done I could see why you were so pissed.

We got wasted at Bunko and I suggested we make that frog disappear for good. So, someone—not me, I don't know who —must have heard me because the frog is gone."

"You don't know where it is?"

"I haven't got a clue."

I smiled. "Well, that sucks for Doris, I guess."

"She is beside herself. She's knocking on everyone's door demanding her frog. She says she can't move without it."

I snorted. "Oh, well." For once I did not have even a twinge of pain for Doris. She didn't deserve my sympathy. "Do you really not know where it is?"

"I really don't," Louise said. "I even checked my roof."

———

Several years later I was driving through Doris's old neighborhood and I saw a house with a badly dressed frog on the front porch holding balloons exclaiming, "Lordy Lordy Look Who's 40!" I can't say for sure that was Doris's frog, but I sure hope it was because fuck Doris and her frog.

THE WRITING YEARS

## CHAPTER 16

### THANK YOU, ELF ON THE SHELF, YOU LITTLE BASTARD

I FOUND my latest (and hopefully last) job in 2011. The Hubs and I were making the real estate thing happen and we'd even managed to stay married. We were both working from home and he was my only coworker—unless you counted the two needy kids demanding to be fed all the time. Before that, I'd always thought that working from home sounded like a dream job. If I didn't have clients to see, I would never have to put on real pants or shower if I didn't want to. Bras were never required and brushing my hair was optional. I could even work from my bed if I wanted! I had dreams of working while my children played quietly and happily at my feet. I could set the real estate world on fire and be Super Mom all at once while wearing yesterday's jammies. Because when you work from home you can balance it all, damn it!

Only problem was I was lonely. The Hubs was great, but 24/7 of the Hubs was *a lot* of quality time with the Hubs, y'know? "Absence makes the heart grow fonder" and all that stuff is true. And then there were my kids. I mean, I loved my kids, but at six and four they were still a handful.

They still demanded a lot of attention (kids say they want to watch *Caillou* all day, but when they're given that option they also realize he's a whiny dick), they couldn't wipe their asses properly, and playing quietly and happily at my feet wasn't happening. They wanted to get out of the house. They wanted to go to parks, museums, the library—anywhere that wasn't our house.

I had taken on all the listings and a lot of that work could be done over the phone or email. The Hubs was the buyer's agent, so he spent more time with people and got to go to lunch with adults and chat with them while I slurped cold mac and cheese off princess plates.

Working from home also sucks because when you're juggling your work and kids, there's also the laundry nagging you and the crumbs on the floor daring you to ignore them another day. The house gets trashed incredibly fast when everyone is there all day long. I was drowning in toys, decrees from my children and the Hubs, and laundry. So much fucking laundry. (For a group of people who didn't get out of our jammies very often, I was shocked how much laundry we could accumulate.)

On top of all of this, I've always been a venty, complainy person, and work had always been a good place to go to decompress. There was always someone at work willing to listen to me or to commiserate with me. I could hang out by the watercooler and bitch to my heart's content and then head back to my cubicle, vented and ready to work. When you work from home with your husband and two small children as your only coworkers, there is no one who will listen to you. So I found myself just talking into what I thought was a black hole.

Turns out, the Hubs had been listening. He had stayed

silent, refusing to encourage me, but after a few years of this setup, the Hubs put his foot down.

"Enough," he said. "I can't take any more."

"Enough?" I asked, perturbed that he'd interrupted an epic Kathie Lee and Hoda rant—I mean, really, did they need to be hammered by ten in the morning every single day? I was pretty sure they were alcoholics and they needed the network to stage an intervention or something, not give them another hour.

"You've got to stop, Jen. It's like this every day. You never stop bitching."

I was shocked. And slightly offended. What the hell? It wasn't like I was bitching at him, which I should have been doing, because unloading everything from the dishwasher to the counter doesn't count as unloading the dishwasher, Hubs. That's just bullshit and you know it. "Well, I'm sorry I have strong opinions on things!" I said. "You knew this when you married me."

"There are people with strong opinions, Jen, and then there's you. You have a strong opinion on everything. You bitched for an hour yesterday about a bib that broke when you put it on Adolpha."

"Well it was absolute crap."

"It was six years old and it's been through two kids! It was two bucks from Walmart. What did you expect?"

"I'm surprised you're not on my side with that one," I argued. "Because now I have to buy a new bib and you hate when I spend money."

"I'm just saying, everything pisses you off, Jen."

"I'm not the only one who feels this way," I said. "I'm sure there are lots of people out there with strong opinions."

"No one except you has strong opinions about Hoda and Kathie Lee."

I scowled. "You don't know that."

"Well, what I do know is that we're home together all day, every day. The kids are driving me crazy and the house is falling apart and all you want to talk about is how pissed off you are at bibs that fall apart and newscasters who have no idea you're alive, and celebrities who don't care what you think of them. Oh, and the mom in the drop-off line who took too long yesterday."

"Well, you should have seen her. She got out of her car to have a full-on conversation with the woman in front of me. There's a whole line of people waiting and they spent five minutes doing nothing except flapping their gums and flipping their hair—I ask you, who has a kindergartner and time to straighten her hair every morning? I barely get my teeth brushed! And then! I swear she got out her phone and showed that bitch pictures of her spring break vacation or something."

"Why didn't anyone honk?"

"Because they're fucking sheep. They don't want to make waves. They sit there and say, 'Oh well, I'm sure it was important.' Bullshit. Take your meetup to Starbucks, ladies! Some of us have places to be. It was so annoying. She's lucky I didn't run her over."

"Yes, so lucky," the Hubs said sarcastically.

"What's that supposed to mean?" I demanded.

"Come on, Jen. You're all bark and no bite. You talk so tough, but you've never been in a fight in your life."

I pouted. He was absolutely right. I'm like that feisty little Chihuahua who thinks she can kick a Great Dane's ass. "Well, I can't help it that I'm so annoyed by people," I whined.

"No, you can't. But I also can't help it that I can't listen anymore. We have to find a solution. You need to bitch and I need some quiet."

"I'll try to do better," I said.

"How about you start a blog?" he suggested.

I wrinkled my nose. "A blog?" I asked.

I didn't know anything about blogging except that my sister-in-law Ida had a blog. She wrote on it daily and she let strangers read her most private thoughts. She talked about these internet people like they were friends and she'd say stuff to me like, "Oh, if you read my blog then you'd know what I'm up to."

I was like, *I don't read your blog because I talk to you.* She was even talking about attending a conference over the summer where she'd meet these internet people for real. I couldn't even imagine. It sounded creepy as hell. Who would want to hang out online all day interacting with perfect strangers? "No, thank you."

"Hang on, just listen. I think a blog would be good for you. It could be an outlet for all your..."

"Rage?"

"Strong opinions," the Hubs said. "You have a degree in creative writing. You keep telling me that you're going to write a book. You're supposed to write a book so you can throw it in Randall's face."

"That fucker," I muttered.

"Well, are you ever going to do it, Jen?"

"I will! I don't have time right now," I argued. "I'm just a little busy running a real estate empire and taking care of two kids and being a fucking amazing wife to you!"

The Hubs snorted.

"It's totally on my life goals," I said. "I will get to it."

"Okay, well, a blog would give you some experience

writing. You could work out the kinks on your blog, do some venting, and maybe figure out what you want to write."

"I already know what I want to write," I said.

"You do?"

"Yes, I'm going to be like Donna Tartt. I'm going to write this *ah-may-zing* and incredible debut novel that stuns everyone with my character development, plot, and prose and then disappear like a recluse."

"Wow, Jen, that is very specific," the Hubs said.

I shrugged. "It's what you do when you're serious about your craft. You don't write a *blog*," I sneered.

The Hubs raised his hands in surrender. He was irritated. "You know what? Fine. Whatever. I'm just trying to help you. But stop complaining to me. That's all I ask."

I stayed quiet for a moment. Normally, I'd fight back and tell the Hubs that I could too be Donna Tartt and I don't appreciate your tone of voice and by the way your dishwasher-emptying skills suck! But I didn't. I could see he was sick of me. He'd had enough. I was driving him insane. I needed to at least try what he suggested or else I needed to contact a divorce attorney. "What would I even call my blog?" I asked softly.

"What?" he said, surprised.

"You need a snappy title. Like Ida's. Hers is 'Ida Wanna Grow Up.' I need something like that. A blog name is the most important thing you can write. People judge it immediately."

"That's easy," the Hubs said. "Yours would be 'People I Want to Punch in the Throat.'"

"What?" I said.

The Hubs shrugged. "You say it all the time and it's definitely snappy. Or should I say punchy?"

I smiled. "It is. You know why it's the throat, right?"

He sighed heavily. "Yes, the nose is clichéd."

"And it's funnier. Plus, I'm so short, the throat is all I can reach. And punch in the junk is crass."

The Hubs snorted. "Yes, let's not let anyone ever think you're crass, Jen."

"I'm a fucking lady, asshole," I replied.

"Well, get started," he said.

"Wait. How do I do it?" I asked.

"I don't know. Just do what you always do when you're not sure. Google that shit."

And so I did. I figured out how to create a blog and buy a URL (surprisingly, People I Want to Punch in the Throat-dot-com was still available!!) and I started venting my spleen. Over the next few months I found my voice and I amassed what I considered to be a decent following: seventy readers who were either related to me or knew me in person.

That was April, and before I knew it December had rolled around. We were up to our eyeballs in holiday kid stuff. Merry memory-making and all that shit. The kids and I baked horrible-looking cookies and I had lost an important Santa gift, so I was turning the house upside down looking for it. The Hubs still hadn't hung our outside lights and we were arguing over whether or not it should even be done that year. Both of the kids still believed in Santa and a friend had kindly given us this magical creature called an Elf on the Shelf. He was an adorable little doll that watches your every move and reports back to Santa. He was supposed to be a game-changer. The kids would fall into line anytime you mentioned the Elf was watching. But in order to make the magic work, a parent had to move the little bastard every night from one shelf to the next.

We were about a week into December and it was a cold

and blustery night. I had just settled into my warm bed when I remembered the damn doll. "Hey." I nudged the Hubs with my cold feet. "The Elf needs to move."

"Okay," he replied, "then go and move it."

"Come on," I whined. "Can't you do it tonight?"

"Nope. I told you we shouldn't lie to them but you insisted upon it, so now it's up to you to keep the lies going." The Hubs is a truther. He hates that the fat guy gets all the credit for the "good" gifts.

"The lies are fun," I argued.

"Fun? Are you having fun right now begging me to move that stupid thing? Was it fun when we were up at midnight on Christmas Eve last year building a play kitchen because Santa delivers toys assembled? Was it fun when you wrote and mailed out a bullshit letter bragging about our boring life to three hundred people who don't care?"

"Wait. Are you suggesting my Christmas letter is a lie?"

"I'm suggesting you embellished it a bit and only showed the good parts of our lives. What was it you said when I got laid off a few years ago?"

"I said that I needed some help with the real estate business and we knew that your gifts and talents were being wasted at your job and so you parted ways amicably."

"Ha! About twenty-four hours before I was asked to part ways. See? Lies. Everyone tells lies."

"Sometimes you have to. Not everyone can be as painfully honest as you! For instance, when someone asks you if you like their hair or car or house, you must say yes. Every single time."

"Even if it's ugly?" The Hubs looked confused.

"Yes, especially when it's ugly. They're not really asking for your opinion."

"Fine. I'll lie to strangers, but I'm sick of lying to our

kids. Don't move the Elf. Let him sit there and we'll tell the kids the truth at breakfast."

I was horrified. "You're a monster," I said, throwing off the covers. "They're too little to know the truth!"

The Hubs shrugged. "I never believed in Santa and I turned out just fine."

"That's debatable," I said, shivering.

I ran into the kitchen and tried to remember what shelf the Elf was lounging on. I only had three shelves that he rotated through, so I found him fairly quickly. I was just going to return to bed when I saw my cell phone on the counter. *I should tell the world I moved my Elf,* I thought. *Because if I don't tell the world, then it didn't really happen. I need a pat on the back and an attagirl for being a good mom.* So I grabbed my phone and wrote a quick update to Facebook:

*It's the first week of December and I'm already forgetting to move my Elf on the Shelf. Please tell me I'm not alone.*

Even though it was close to midnight, I got several responses immediately:

*Oh shit, I forgot that thing. Thanks for the reminder.*

*Dang it. Moving him now.*

*Crap. What a PITA. Going to move him.*

*Done! But only because I just remembered like five minutes ago.*

It was crazy. I couldn't believe how many Good-Enough Mothers there were besides me! I was just feeling a cozy warmth of mediocre sisterhood washing over me when another response popped up:

*Wow. I can't believe how hard you're making this, moms. You just need a system!*

*A system?* I thought. *Who does she think she is?!* I was furious. This helpful tidbit of advice was from Velma. Velma was a chick who had no children. No, that's not true. She had *dog* children. Just ask her and she'd tell you how taking care of her two dogs was just like taking care of kids. Umm, no, Velma, it's not even close. You go to work all day and leave your dogs in a cage. I can't do that with my kids, because they're human beings! I was ready to tell her to go take her dogs for a long walk off a short pier when she dumped another nugget of wisdom on us:

*I did a quick search and came up with this great list of ideas! You moms should maybe get off Facebook and take this lady's advice, just saying!*

"Just sayin'," I seethed. "Ha. That's the fuck you of sanctimonious bitches."

I was thinking of a thousand different scathing responses I could come up with for Velma when my friend Dawn replied:

*Have you looked at this "helpful" list, Jen? It has a hundred and one ideas for what to do with your Elf on the Shelf. Who needs a hundred and one ideas? There are only twenty-five days of Christmas!*

This comment stopped me from planning Velma's epic takedown and forced me to really look at what she'd shared. You see, I loved Dawn, but she was an overachiever of the highest level. Dawn had produced so much breast milk with her kids that she donated it to a homeless shelter and they actually took it. Dawn makes homemade everything, including birthday cakes, and it's always organic and preferably from ingredients she and her adorable children harvested from their backyard or the closest co-op orchard. Dawn uses every opportunity to teach her children something about science or math or reading. ("Let's multiply all the numbers of the license plate in front of us, kids!") Dawn's home is a showstopper and I've never once seen a dirty sock—let alone dirty undies—tucked into the cushions of her sofa. In short, Dawn is perfect. And if she thought the list was over the top, then it must be.

I clicked the link and I was immediately accosted by a bright and friendly blog inviting me to subscribe and follow along. Beautiful pictures of a cute but naughty elf adorned the site, and I scanned the list. Helpful tips like:

*Trash your kitchen making Christmas cookies and say the Elf did it, teeheehee!* and *Swap all of the clothes from one kid's closet to the other while they're sleeping!*

jumped out at me immediately.

"What the fuck is this nonsense?" I muttered. "Who has time for this shit? My kitchen is already trashed enough. Why would I create more work for myself? I just need to move the Elf from one shelf to the next, not roll out a red carpet for him." I took a closer look. "Holy shit, she has instructions to make a red carpet for the Elf. No, fuck this lady."

I don't know what exactly came over me at that moment. It was late, I was exhausted, I had another never-ending day of drama and work ahead of me, and the last thing I needed was this list to make me feel less than.

"I'm a good mom," I said to my filthy kitchen. "This is bullshit!"

I grabbed my laptop and sat down on the floor. I wrote an angry, passionate tirade about the Elf on the Shelf. I just let it all bubble out. I was thinking of the perky blogger and her one hundred and one ideas and how she must just assume that I have nothing better to do than destroy feather pillows or make Elf-size parachutes out of underwear. *No, no, no, no!* I thought as I banged away on my keyboard. I thought about Velma and her condescending attitude toward moms who were just trying to do their best. My kids were fed, they were warm, they were loved, they were happy! Fuck Velma!

"When she has a baby I'm going to send her an Elf on the Shelf as a gift," I said. "That'll show her. Let's see her try this shit!"

I don't remember how long it took me to write, but I know it wasn't that long. The words just flowed out of me, and my fingers flew across the keyboard. I was possessed. When I was done, I hit publish and shared it with my friends on Facebook and immediately went to bed.

The next morning I checked my blog stats and like always I had about three hundred reads on the piece. I was quite proud of myself. That was a good number for me. I went about my life and really didn't think about the blog entry for a few more days. I was too busy trying to remember to move my Elf and find that damn Santa present that I'd hidden just a little too well. If I needed any kind of system, it was a system for keeping track of presents!

A week later I was in the middle of a PTA meeting. I was the president. (Of course I was—I'm an absolute control freak who likes things done her way.) I was about halfway through the agenda when the Hubs texted me.

Hubs: *Something up w/ur blog.*
Me: *What u mean?*
Hubs: *Lots of people reading elf on shelf.*
Me: *Hmm. Really? Dawn shared it, maybe it's her friends. Probably pissed off since they're overachievers.*
Hubs: *No, it's more than that. A lot a lot. 3k people on there right now.*
Me: *What? No. That's mistake. Ur reading it wrong.*
Hubs: *Am not. Now it's 3.5k, 4k. WTF?*
Me: *I think stats are broken. Gotta go, PTA mtg. Everyone waiting for me.*
Hubs: *OK*

I went on with the meeting, and about fifteen minutes later my phone buzzed again.

Hubs: *10k*

A few minutes later:

Hubs: *25k!!! Something is happening here!!!*

I nudged my friend sitting next to me and showed her my phone. "Check this out, there are twenty-five thousand people on my blog right now."

"Your punch thing?" she asked, surprised.

"Yeah. Strange, huh? It's got to be a glitch, right?"

She shrugged. "Who knows?"

"Okay, where were we?" I asked the group. "Um, treasury report, maybe?" I had lost track of the agenda completely.

"New business, Jen," the treasurer said.

"Right!" I said. "Okay, any new bus—" My phone buzzed.

Hubs: *100K!!! WTF IS GOING ON???*

My palms were too sweaty and my hands were too shaky to text back. I wanted to yell, "Meeting's adjourned, bitches, I'm going viral!" but instead I asked calmly, "Any new business?" I waited a full ten seconds before I said, "No? Nothing? Okay, great, meeting's adjourned. See you next month" and ran out of the building.

I rushed home and found the Hubs hunched over my laptop. "I'm watching real-time Google analytics and it's crazy. Thousands of people are on the site. And then after they read the Elf on the Shelf, they read everything. They're going back to the beginning and starting from your very first post."

I felt a little queasy. "Maybe it's a mistake," I said.

The Hubs shook his head. "No, check your inbox. You have hundreds of comments and tons of emails from people."

"Really? Like, strangers?"

"Yes, of course, Jen!"

"Let me see." I snatched the laptop from him and opened the email at the top. I read aloud, "'Dear Jen, You are a terrible mother and I can't even believe that you're allowed to have children. You're also clearly jealous of this other blogger and the fact that she is a better mother than you. You are awful. Someone should take away your kids!'" I could feel the freak-out coming on. "Oh my God! She hates me! Take it down! Take it down! She wants to steal my kids!"

The Hubs grabbed the computer. "No, she's just one person. Look, there are so many more positive ones. Here, listen to this. 'Jen, thank you for making me feel like I am not alone. I try so hard to be a good mom and I feel like everything I see on the internet tells me that I'm doing it wrong. You are a breath of fresh air.'"

I calmed down a bit. "Okay, yeah, that's a good one."

"Or how about: 'Dear Jen, You say all the things I think. Thank you for speaking for the rest of us.'"

"Yeah, I like that one too," I admitted.

"Sure, there are some shitty emails and comments. But I've read them all, and believe me, the positive outweigh the negative. You've done it, Jen. You've found your people."

"Whoa." I read some more emails and comments. Most of them were great, but I was really scared of the few women (and the occasional man) who threatened to steal my kids in order to give them a better life. I quickly scrubbed my blog of all identifying names or information and gave my kids the fakest, worst-est names I could think of: Gomer and Adolpha. (To this day, I get the most hate mail about their fake names. People think Gomer is a nimrod and I must love Adolph Hitler. Idiots.) The Hubs and I made a pact that night to never reveal their names or post pictures of their faces. I also created a Facebook page for People I Want to Punch in the Throat. I had a lot of people trying to be my friend on Facebook and I was way too scared to accept them.

We stayed there watching the numbers climb. I'm not sure what we fed our kids for dinner or if we actually fed them at all (I hope they ate that night. Surely they did. They would have cried for food, right?), but it was around bedtime when the Hubs said, "Well, there it is. One million reads."

"What?"

"You just got one million reads on the Elf on the Shelf. You hit it in less than a day."

I was a bundle of emotions. I was happy, scared, thrilled, terrified, excited, confused, and shocked. "I need a paper bag to breathe into," I gasped. "That's so many people."

The Hubs smiled. "Yes, it is."

"I didn't mean for it to be read by so many people," I said. "It's not perfect. It's not any good."

"Jen, it's fine. You obviously hit a nerve. The biggest question is, what are you going to write for tomorrow?"

"Tomorrow?" I asked.

"Yeah. How many people are on your new Facebook page?"

"About seventeen thousand."

"Seventeen thousand people, Jen. They've read everything you've written. I told you, they were reading the archives."

"Yeah, but I mean, I'll never write anything as popular as the Elf again," I moaned.

The Hubs shrugged. "No, probably not. But who cares? Jen, the first night we met you told me you wanted to be a writer. Here is your chance. Lightning has struck for you. The opportunity is in front of you, but you're going to have to work hard to really make it a career. Do you want writing to be your career?"

"Yes," I said weakly. "I think so." I thought about my asshole college advisor, Randall, and I was immediately seized with fear. I thought about the horrible things he'd said to me about my writing. The predictions he'd made about my future. I felt like maybe he knew something I didn't. Maybe this was a fluke and everyone would be gone by morning.

"Well, you can leverage this. You've got seventeen thousand people waiting to read whatever you come up with next."

My heart sank. "What could I possibly write now?" I asked. "I don't have any ideas!"

"I don't know, but I bet it will be great," he said, getting up to leave.

"Wait! Where are you going?" I asked.

"I'm going to put the kids to bed. I can't wait to see what you do next," he said.

I sat down and stared at the blank screen. I felt self-doubt creeping in. Randall was right. *I don't have anything to say!* I thought sadly. But then I read through a few more emails and I felt my confidence surge. I thought about Randall's smug face and how I wanted to send him my best-selling book, autographed and encouraging him to shove the book up his ass. I was fueled by my readers' support and my need to prove Randall wrong. I ignored my churning stomach and I started typing.

I wrote about the damn Christmas lights that still weren't hung up outside.

No, it didn't get a million hits, but it did get a lot and it started me on the path toward a career in writing. A career that the week before I'd considered a distant and impossible dream. Over the next several years I wrote hundreds more blog posts, won tons of awards, and gained close to a million followers on social media. And then finally, I wrote a book that hit the *New York Times* Best Sellers list.

I know what you're wondering right now: *So did you send the book to Randall, Jen?*

I didn't. Randall had pissed me off and motivated me, but I didn't want to give him the satisfaction of knowing that his words meant anything to me, let alone inspired me in some weird way. Words have power when you let them, and I refused to give Randall and his words any power over me. My years of blogging and hearing countless times how much my opinions and my writing (and my kids' names) sucked taught me not to care anymore what people thought of me. Criticism rolls off me now and I am bolstered by the strength of my tribe. It was freeing to let go of that worry and to focus only on the three people in my life whose opinions actually count: the Hubs, Gomer, and Adolpha. Those are the only opinions that I consider, and as long as they like what I do, then I'm happy.

## ACKNOWLEDGMENTS

Thank you, thank you, thank you to everyone who makes it possible for me to work from home in my pajamas. I'm not cut out for an office job anymore!

Thank you to my husband for letting me air our dirty laundry. Thank you for making sure our kids get fed when I'm on a deadline. Thank you for talking me off ledges and keeping me sane. Thank you for always supporting me and my dreams.

Thank you to my kids who put up with having a weird mom who spends all day hidden in the basement talking to strangers on the internet. Thanks for sharing me.

Thank you to my amazing and talented cover designer, J Caleb. I'm so happy you get me because half the time I don't even know what I want.

Thank you to my fabulous editor, Julia Ganis. When I heard you speak a few years ago I knew we had to work together, and I'm so glad we did. Thank you for laughing at the right moments and pointing out my lack of grammar.

Thank you to Elizabeth Catalano and her eagle eyes.

Thank you to everyone who leaves me reviews and follows me on social media. You are the best coworkers I've ever had.

# ABOUT THE AUTHOR

JEN MANN is best known for her wildly popular and hysterical blog People I Want to Punch in the Throat. She has been described by many as Erma Bombeck—with f-bombs. Jen is the author of the *New York Times* bestseller *People I Want to Punch in the Throat: Competitive Crafters, Drop-Off Despots, and Other Suburban Scourges* which was a Finalist for a Goodreads Reader's Choice Award. Her latest book, *My Lame Life: Queen of the Misfits*, is her first book of fiction for young adults.

Jen is a married mother of two children whom she calls Gomer and Adolpha in her writings—she swears their real names are actually worse.

*Follow Jen everywhere and subscribe to her newsletter.*

www.jenmannwrites.com

ALSO BY JEN MANN

My Lame Life: Queen of the Misfits

People I Want to Punch in the Throat: Competitive Crafters, Drop-Off Despots, and Other Suburban Scourges

Spending the Holidays with People I Want to Punch in the Throat: Yuletide Yahoos, Ho-Ho-Humblebraggers, and Other Seasonal Scourges

But Did You Die?

I Just Want to Be Perfect

I STILL Just Want to Pee Alone

I Just Want to Be Alone

I Just Want to Pee Alone

Just a Few People I Want to Punch in the Throat (Vols. 1-6)

Thank you for reading my books. I appreciate your support and I hope you enjoyed them. I also hope you will tell a friend—or thirty—about them. Please do me a huge favor and leave me a review.

71196467R10135

Made in the USA
San Bernardino, CA
13 March 2018